S. Hrg. 114–620

THE CURRENT STATE OF RESEARCH, DIAGNOSIS, AND TREATMENT FOR POST–TRAUMATIC STRESS DISORDER AND TRAUMATIC BRAIN INJURY

HEARING

BEFORE THE

SUBCOMMITTEE ON STRATEGIC FORCES

OF THE

COMMITTEE ON ARMED SERVICES
UNITED STATES SENATE

ONE HUNDRED FOURTEENTH CONGRESS

SECOND SESSION

APRIL 20, 2016

Printed for the use of the Committee on Armed Services

Available via the World Wide Web: http://www.fdsys.gov/

U.S. GOVERNMENT PUBLISHING OFFICE

25–235 PDF   WASHINGTON : 2017

For sale by the Superintendent of Documents, U.S. Government Publishing Office
Internet: bookstore.gpo.gov   Phone: toll free (866) 512–1800; DC area (202) 512–1800
Fax: (202) 512–2104   Mail: Stop IDCC, Washington, DC 20402–0001

CONTENTS

APRIL 20, 2016

THE CURRENT STATE OF RESEARCH, DIAGNOSIS, AND TREATMENT FOR POST-TRAUMATIC STRESS DISORDER AND TRAUMATIC BRAIN INJURY

WEDNESDAY, APRIL 20, 2016

U.S. SENATE,
SUBCOMMITTEE ON PERSONNEL,
COMMITTEE ON ARMED SERVICES,
Washington, DC.

The subcommittee met, pursuant to notice, at 2:36 p.m. in Room SR–222, Russell Senate Office Building, Senator Lindsey O. Graham (chairman of the subcommittee) presiding.

Committee members present: Senators Graham, Cotton, Tillis, Sullivan, Gillibrand, Blumenthal, and King.

OPENING STATEMENT OF SENATOR LINDSEY GRAHAM

Senator GRAHAM. The hearing will come to order.

We're here to receive testimony on research, diagnosis, and treatment of post-traumatic stress and traumatic brain injury in the Department of Defense and Department of Veterans Affairs.

The committee meets this afternoon to receive testimony from the Department of Defense and Department of Veterans Affairs on research, diagnosis, and treatment of post-traumatic stress and traumatic brain injury. This is an important hearing. We must do everything we can to help servicemen and women and veterans suffering from PTS [post-traumatic stress] and TBI [Traumatic Brain Injury].

We're fortunate to have a distinguished panel of witnesses joining us today: Captain Walter Green—say it——

Captain GREENHALGH. Greenhalgh.

Senator GILLIBRAND.—Greenhalgh, sorry about that—Medical Corps, United States Navy, Director for the National Intrepid Center of Excellence at Walter Reed National Military Medical Center; Captain Mike Colston, Medical Corps, United States Navy, Director of the Defense Center of Excellence for Psychological Health and Traumatic Brain Injury; and Dr. Amy Street, Deputy Director of the Women's Health Division, National Center for Post-Traumatic Stress, Department of Veterans Affairs.

Post-traumatic stress and traumatic brain injury have been called the signature wounds of the Afghan and Iraq conflict. Since 2001, about 5 percent of the over 2.7 million servicemembers deployed in support of the wars in Afghanistan and Iraq were diagnosed with PTS. And from 2000 through September 2015, there are

(1)

over 339,000 TBI cases diagnosed, with most of these being mild TBI diagnosed in garrison locations. With the significant impacts that both PTS and TBI have made on our servicemembers and veterans, it is vitally important that we better understand, through well-developed medical research, the causes of PTS and TBI, and develop appropriate measures to treat and eventually prevent PTS and TBI. While both DOD [Department of Defense] and VA [Veterans Affairs] have made significant research investments to learn more about PTS and TBI leading to major advancements in diagnosis and treatments, more work must be done on prevention.

Today, I want our witnesses to tell us what DOD and the VA are doing to prevent, diagnose, and treat PTS and TBI, and to give us an overview of promising treatments, therapies, and technologies that may be available in the near future. Finally, tell us what this subcommittee can do to help your department provide better care for servicemen and women and veterans who may suffer from PTS and TBI.

Senator Gillibrand.

STATEMENT OF SENATOR KIRSTEN E. GILLIBRAND

Senator GILLIBRAND. Thank you so much, Chairman Graham, for your leadership. I'm so grateful I get to serve on this subcommittee with you.

Senator GRAHAM. Thank you.

Senator GILLIBRAND. It's extremely meaningful, the work that we do.

I want to welcome our witnesses. Thank you for your service, and thank you for the focus you have on the state of research, diagnosis, and treatment for post-traumatic stress disorder and traumatic brain injury.

I'm pleased we have witnesses here, both from the DOD and the Department of Veterans Affairs. Both of these agencies are addressing significant caseloads of PTSD and TBI. I look forward to learning about how each agency responds to the challenges of research treating these conditions, and if there are different approaches in how to do this. Although PTSD and TBI are widely recognized as signature wounds of our recent conflict in Iraq and Afghanistan, we know that these conditions are more than just war injuries. We know that PTSD is triggered by a traumatic event. That traumatic event can be combat-related, but all too frequently, the trigger event can be military sexual assault. While we continue our efforts to rid the military of this scourge, we must provide world-class treatment to the survivors of this horrendous crime.

I am particularly interested in learning more about PTSD that is caused by sexual assaults. Specifically, I would like to know if PTSD presents itself differently in male survivors versus female survivors, and how treatment for PTSD meets the unique needs of male survivors of sexual assault.

I'd also like to hear more about the state of the art in diagnosing and treating PTSD and TBI, the interaction between the two, and the ongoing research to improve diagnosis and treatment of these conditions. Over the years, our understanding of PTSD and TBI has grown substantially; however, there remains much more to be learned.

Furthermore, we need to ensure that those who suffer from PTSD and TBI related to military service have access to a healthcare system that is able to meet their physical and mental healthcare needs. Our servicemembers, retirees, and their families deserve the highest-quality care.

So, thank you each to our witnesses for the time and effort they've put into this important issue.

Thank you.

Senator GRAHAM. Well, one, thank you for the compliment, Senator Gillibrand. It's been a pleasure working with you and your staff.

Captain, please.

STATEMENT OF CAPTAIN WALTER M. GREENHALGH, MC, USN, DIRECTOR FOR THE NATIONAL INTREPID CENTER OF EXCELLENCE DIRECTORATE, WALTER REED NATIONAL MILITARY MEDICAL CENTER

Captain GREENHALGH. Well, good afternoon, sir. Thank you.

Well, good afternoon, Chairman Graham, Ranking Member Gillibrand, and members of the subcommittee. Thank you all for the opportunity to discuss with you the Department of Defense's efforts to prevent, diagnose, treat, and research traumatic brain injury, or TBI, and its associated psychological health comorbidities.

As the Director for the National Intrepid Center of Excellence, or NICoE, at the Walter Reed National Military Medical Center in Bethesda, I lead a team of exceptional professionals whose mission is to improve the lives of patients and families impacted by TBI and psychological health issues.

Through the generosity of the American people and the Intrepid Fallen Heroes Fund, NICoE opened in 2010 on the Walter Reed Bethesda campus, followed by five of the proposed nine Intrepid Spirit Centers, or NICoE satellites, to be build on military installations around the country. Together, we've created an integrated TBI care network. It's a very important component of the military health system's TBI pathway of care, as managed by the Defense and Veterans Brain Injury Center.

This past year, NICoE officially transitioned into the Walter Reed National Military Medical Center command structure, becoming a directorate within the flagship of military medicine and formalizing research support and collaboration from the Uniformed Services University of the Health Sciences, also on the Bethesda campus.

This completely integrated approach to our work, leveraging the expertise and resources of Walter Reed's outpatient TBI programs, inpatient consultation service, and Uniformed Services University's research capabilities allows us to serve our unique patient population in a seamless fashion, using the entire TBI care portfolio available on America's Academic Health Campus in Bethesda.

An important part of the Federal TBI continuum of care in the TBI research mission—is the TBI research mission. NICoE and the network of military health system TBI Care Centers, in collaboration with partners, including the Veterans Administration, National Institutes of Health, Uniformed Services University, and other Federal academic and private institutions, continue to push the boundaries of innovation with cutting-edge translational research.

One signature collaborative project is the congressionally mandated longitudinal 15-year study to comprehensively categorize servicemembers and their caregivers affected by TBI. Another example is the neuroimaging core research project, with over 1,000 servicemembers affected by TBR thus far evaluated clinically and with state-of-the-art neuroimaging capability, collecting over 40,000 imaging and clinical datapoints for study per patient.

In addition to our high-tech research, NICoE is actively engaged in clinical research on our high-touch aspects of our program, such as our National Endowment for the Arts-supported Therapeutic Arts Program and our congressionally supported research on Kindergarten-9 assisted therapy. And by tracking both the short- and long-term outcomes of our programs, we are also able to rapidly assess and accelerate discovery more effectively using every taxpayer dollar by putting the research and its findings immediately to use at the deckplates amongst our patients.

So, I'm grateful for the opportunity to represent the men and women working at NICoE, as well as the patients we're honored to serve. I look forward to answering your questions today.

Thank you.

[The joint prepared statement of Captain Greenhalgh and Captain Colston follows:]

JOINT PREPARED STATEMENT BY CAPTAIN MIKE COLSTON, M.D. AND CAPTAIN WALTER GREENHALGH, M.D.

Chairman Graham, Ranking Member Gillibrand and members of the Committee, we are pleased to discuss the Department of Defense's (DOD) efforts to promote psychological health (PH) and prevent, diagnose, and treat traumatic brain injury (TBI) and behavioral health conditions. We are honored to be joined by Dr. Amy Street, the Deputy Director of the Department of Veteran Affairs' (VA) National Center for Post-Traumatic Stress Disorder's (PTSD) Women's Health Sciences Division.

We want to thank the Committee for its sustained leadership and support for the work we perform in the Military Health System (MHS) to care for our Nation's Service members, veterans, and their families—especially those dealing with the complex issues of PH and TBI. Your investments in medical research have led to important advancements in care and a greater understanding of where future research should be targeted.

Advances in combat medicine and protective equipment have saved the lives of countless Service men and women who would have died from their injuries in conflicts of the past. With that welcome increase in survival rates, however, comes a lifelong obligation to Service members whose road to recovery, both physical and mental, is long. By their nature, the signature invisible wounds of our recent wars—PTSD and TBI—demand greater sensitivity in identification of the injury or illness, as well as an ability to coordinate treatment with other injuries.

Over the last 15 years over 300,000 Service members have suffered a TBI and over one million have been treated for behavioral health conditions. To meet these challenges, we have expanded the ability of our military hospitals, military clinics and network of civilian providers to treat these conditions, introduced new therapies to improve recovery, and generated a comprehensive portfolio of research efforts to advance the state of the science and drive evolution of care.

Although our recent conflicts have added greater awareness and urgency to understanding PH and TBI, these medical conditions are not confined to military personnel alone. That is why the DOD has partnered with other government agencies, academic research institutions, and the private sector to share what we know and what we have learned, address our gaps in knowledge, and increase our collaboration on research. Many of the efforts and milestones that will be discussed today are a result of this ongoing collaborative work.

CURRENT STATE OF TBI/PH RESEARCH, TREATMENT, AND THERAPIES

TBI and PH research represent complex undertakings, as these conditions are heterogeneous and often associated with other medical conditions. Our research often involves differentiating comorbidities like PTSD, depression, substance abuse, and chronic pain—all factors which can complicate the prevention and treatment of other PH conditions and TBI. The best way to account for these comorbidities, and effectively identify treatments and therapies, is through the kinds of comprehensive and longitudinal research efforts we have undertaken. What we've learned about the brain over the past decade of PH and TBI research outpaces any advancement of knowledge to date—and only through continued effort will we reap the benefits of the research we have begun.

The President's Executive Order in 2012 directed Federal agencies to develop a coordinated National Research Action Plan (NRAP). This directive has accelerated the knowledge we have gained and strengthened inter-agency cooperation and co-ordination. The DOD, VA, and Department of Health and Human Services (HHS), responded to the Executive Order with a wide-reaching plan to improve scientific understanding, develop effective treatment, and reduce occurrences of PTSD, PH conditions, TBI and suicide. The NRAP represents the ten-year strategic blueprint for interagency research to identify and develop more effective diagnostic and treat-ment methodologies to improve outcomes for TBI and PH and we are eager to con-tinue working with our inter-government partners to advance our understanding of these conditions.

Specifically, two jointly funded VA and DOD consortiums are focused on priorities outlined in the NRAP: The Consortium to Alleviate PTSD (CAP), and the Chronic Effects of Neurotrauma Consortium (CENC). The CAP seeks to improve the psycho-logical and physical health and well-being of Operation Enduring Freedom, Iraqi Freedom, and New Dawn Service members and veterans by developing and evalu-ating the most effective preventive, diagnostic, prognostic, treatment and rehabilita-tive strategies for combat-related PH issues and comorbid conditions. The CENC is dedicated to establishing a comprehensive understanding of the chronic sequelae that may be associated with mild TBI. Together, CAP and CENC ensure that high priority research areas are being addressed and efforts are not being duplicated across or within agencies. This collaboration supports a more unified vision for re-search within the federal community to better anticipate and respond to emerging medical requirements.

In 2012, DOD funded an independent study to assess access to mental health pro-viders for more than 1.3 million Service Members and their families who reside in rural and remote locations. Initial results of the study were released in January 2015 and included a geospatial development tool to monitor locations of US military members, their families, and their distance from mental health care. Recommenda-tions emerging from these findings included the increased use of telehealth and other technologies to improve access to care for remote populations. The Department is pursuing the study's recommendations, including incorporating the increased use of telehealth and other technologies to improve access to care for remote popu-lations. We recently updated our policies on telehealth and telemedicine to encour-age greater adoption by both providers and patients and continue work to expand utilization of telemedicine capabilities.

The Department has taken other steps to increase access to needed behavioral health services, and we monitor our performance in access and quality. We have eliminated the limit on inpatient behavioral health bed days in our TRICARE pro-gram, and we are finalizing our policies to ensure alignment with the Mental Health Parity Act in 2016. The MHS is a leader among US health systems in achieving high rates of timely outpatient follow-up visits for patients with PTSD or depression after psychiatric hospitalization for PTSD: 86 percent of patients who were hospital-ized were seen as an outpatient within 7 days of discharge; 95 percent were seen within 30 days. Additionally, 91 percent of patients diagnosed with PTSD and 82 percent of patients with depression received psychotherapy.

The Department has also introduced new approaches to how we screen for TBI in Service Members returning from deployment. Improvements in TBI screening, in-cluding screening in theater, and changes in the post-deployment health assessment and re-assessment were based, in part, on evidence derived from DOD-funded stud-ies.

The use of integrated interdisciplinary treatment programs has also increased since 2007 due to evidence from DOD studies for management of severe TBI and a number of DOD-funded studies are cited by the Joint Theater Trauma System Clinical Practice Guideline Management of Patients with Severe Head Trauma. This highly practical guidance is revised annually and directs care for severe and penetrating TBI sustained in theater.

DOD continues to develop innovative technologies in areas of TBI care that improve recovery and reintegration. Examples of novel interventions for TBI under study include neurofeedback, biofeedback, the interactive metronome, computer-based cognitive rehabilitation, and non-invasive electrical stimulation devices. To identify objective TBI screening, diagnostic, and assessment tools, the DOD is studying the effectiveness of innovative technologies such as portable devices to measure the brain's electrical activity, environmental sensors and other concussion detection systems, and neurocognitive assessment tools.

Current progress in the upstream treatment of PH and TBI is exemplified by the *inTransition* program established in response to Executive Order 13625. The *inTransition* program pairs trained mental health professionals with Service members transitioning to new care teams in VA or in the local community. It has wide utilization—with over 10,000 calls per month and more than 15,000 extended coaching cases since its inception in February 2010. This number will continue to grow as all Service Members who are receiving mental health care and leaving military service are now automatically enrolled into the *inTransition* program. By enhancing coordination between referring and gaining providers, *inTransition* reduced the number of Service Members who disengage from mental health care during a period of change.

In addition to the progress in PH and TBI treatment practices, our physical infrastructure has been expanded and improved over the past five years. The Defense and Veterans Brain Injury Center (DVBIC), National Intrepid Center of Excellence (NICoE), and other Intrepid Sites make up a network of treatment facilities across the world that focus on TBI care for Service members and their families. Located on military installations, providers at these facilities diagnose and initiate the treatment for patients referred with complex, comorbid PH/TBI conditions; conduct focused research, and deliver expert treatments to improve TBI and PH outcomes. These centers leverage their collective reach and provide comprehensive TBI care throughout the MHS.. Additional DVBIC sites located in VA Polytrauma Rehabilitation Centers extend the scope of members and their families. Located on military installations, providers at these facilities diagnose and initiate the treatment for patients referred with complex, comorbid PH/TBI conditions; conduct focused research, and deliver expert treatments to improve TBI and PH outcomes. These centers leverage their collective reach and provide comprehensive TBI care throughout the MHS.. Additional DVBIC sites located in VA Polytrauma Rehabilitation Centers extend the scope of members and their families. Located on military installations, providers at these facilities diagnose and initiate the treatment for patients referred with complex, comorbid PH/TBI conditions; conduct focused research, and deliver expert treatments to improve TBI and PH outcomes. These centers leverage their collective reach and provide comprehensive TBI care throughout the MHS.. Additional DVBIC sites located in VA Polytrauma Rehabilitation Centers extend the scope of

FUTURE OF TBI/PH RESEARCH, TREATMENT, AND THERAPIES

Research has provided many answers and influenced improvements to care—however, gaps remain in the nation's scientific knowledge about PH and TBI, gaps that we are working diligently to address.

Coordinated research efforts to accelerate discovery of the mechanisms underlying behavioral health conditions, TBI, and other comorbidities remain a top priority. Understanding pathophysiology allows researchers to target treatment more efficiently and identify new targets for treatment. Our research plan outlines a timeline to work towards developing effective biomarkers that detect disorders early and accurately. Additionally, the NRAP work group is orchestrating better coordination of federal research strategies and investments. Major efforts include the Federal Interagency TBI Research (FITBIR) Registry to share research data, use of Federal RePORTER and other interagency databases to share research portfolio information, and a Joint Strategic Portfolio Reviews and Analyses to discuss current activities, priorities, and remaining gaps.

In 2001 the DOD initiated the largest longitudinal study of Service Members, Veterans, and their families in US military history—the Millennium Cohort Study. This epidemiological study includes more than 200,000 participants across the globe, with a planned follow-up for 21+ years to evaluate the long-term impact of military experiences during and after the time of military service. The Millennium Cohort Study offers a unique opportunity to define the challenges that Service Members, Veterans and military families experience. This will serve to advance the understanding of protective and vulnerability factors that can then be used to design training and treatment programs into the future.

Our partnership programs also provide us with important insights. Working with the National Collegiate Athletic Association (NCAA), DOD created the Concussion Assessment, Research and Education (CARE) Consortium to conduct a large-scale, multi-site study of the natural history of concussion in both sexes across multiple sports. The aim of the study is to address current gaps in our knowledge, and shed light on the neurobiological mechanisms of concussion symptoms and the trajectory of recovery. It will provide information on a cohort of individuals with SRC, and contribute to other datasets for public use and drive a more informed public discussion about concussion care and policy.

In addition to these advancements made in research, treatment, and therapies—the MHS is working internally to make PH and TBI efforts more effective, cost-efficient, and beneficial to Service Members, Veterans, and their families. DCoE estimates there are more than 200 programs receiving DOD funding to provide both clinical and non-clinical psychological health or TBI services for Service Members and family members. Such services account for more than $1 billion annually. DOD has begun a multifaceted approach to examine program effectiveness to review the value of these programs, ensuring they both are non-duplicative and informed by clinical evidence.

Beginning in fiscal year 2015, DCoE implemented onsite program evaluations with current DOD-funded PH and TBI programs to measure program effectiveness and meet the intent of NDAA [National Defense Authorization Act] directives. DCoE's program evaluation efforts are DOD's primary mechanism to comprehensively document program efficacy within the MHS.

CONCLUSION

Scientific progress is incremental and takes time, but Service Members and their families need solutions. The progress the Department—and the Nation—has made in the past 10 years has led to an expanded knowledge base and cutting-edge treatments that have improved the lives of our Service Members, Veterans, their families, and all Americans. Yet, we are neither complacent nor satisfied with our achievements. Our mission is urgent. We have a long-term plan to continue to improve our treatment of these very complex medical conditions. We are honored to represent the Department of Defense today on behalf of the men and women who conduct such vital research, and deliver care in support of such a special population. We are grateful for the ongoing support of this Committee and the Congress in supporting our efforts, and we look forward to answering your questions.

STATEMENT OF CAPTAIN MICHAEL J. COLSTON, MC, USN, DIRECTOR, DEFENSE CENTERS OF EXCELLENCE FOR PSYCHOLOGICAL HEALTH AND TRAUMATIC BRAIN INJURY

Captain COLSTON. Chairman Graham, Ranking Member Gillibrand, members of the subcommittee, thank you for support of our Nation's servicemembers, veterans, and their families.

I'm pleased to share DOD's efforts to foster research for PTSD and other psychological health conditions, TBI, and comorbidities, including substance-use disorders, pain disorders, and suicide.

Last year, over a quarter of our servicemembers were treated for these conditions, so please allow me to discuss how we evolved to support the need. We reduced barriers to care, including stigma. We expanded access to care by tripling the size of our mental health infrastructure. We improved transition points in the continuum of care. And we improved our system's ability to treat the sickest patients. All the while, we developed a comprehensive research portfolio to study PTSD, TBI, and suicide.

DOD partners with other government agencies, academia, and the private sector in research. The centerpiece of our collaborative efforts is the National Research Action Plan, or NRAP. NRAP brings together DOD, VA, the Department of Health and Human Services, and the Department of Education, improving our understanding of TBI and PTSD. But, there are challenges. One challenge is ascertaining why PTSD, TBI, depression, substance-use disorders, and chronic pain all present together. Longitudinal research efforts, like the Millennium Cohort Study and the 15-year study on TBI, will aid our understanding, just as the Framingham Study helped elucidate factors in cardiovascular disease.

PTSD treatment has a wide evidence base, with A-level evidence supporting the use of therapy and medications for PTSD survivors, irrespective of trauma, be it developmental, be it sexual, or be it from the ravages of war. We, nonetheless, face challenges in how best to structure our health system to support those interventions. Health systems research is imperative. Answering mandates from Congress in NDAAs '13 and '15, agency priority goals, and DOD's Cost Analysis and Program Evaluation Office, my center, the Defense Centers of Excellence for Psychological Health and TBI, is halfway through a 5-year effort to evaluate psychological health in TBI programs for effectiveness, including outcomes and fiscal granularity. Cooperation with academia and federally funded research and development centers aids us in this effort, leading to analyses focused on results.

With your continued support, I'm confident our discoveries will bear fruit in the years ahead. And I look forward to answering your questions.

STATEMENT OF AMY E. STREET, DEPUTY DIRECTOR, WOMEN'S HEALTH SCIENCES DIVISION, NATIONAL CENTER FOR POSTTRAUMATIC STRESS DISORDER

Dr. STREET. Good afternoon, Chairman Graham, Ranking Member Gillibrand, and members of the subcommittee.

As a researcher whose work is focused on military sexual trauma, MST, and a psychologist with the Department of Veterans Affairs who works with veterans who have experienced MST, I am grateful for the opportunity to speak about the current state of research related to MST and the diagnosis and treatment of conditions associated with MST, with a particular focus on post-traumatic stress disorder. I'm also honored to be seated with my colleagues representing the Department of Defense.

Research indicates that experiences of sexual harassment and sexual assault during military service are far too common. Data from the 2014 RAND [Research and Development] Military Workplace Study indicated that 1 percent of servicemen and 5 percent of servicewomen were sexually assaulted in the past year, impacting an estimated 20,300 Active Duty servicemembers. The majority of these assaults occurred in military settings or were perpetrated by military personnel.

Experiences that constitute sexual harassment are even more common, with 7 percent of servicemen and 22 percent of servicewomen experiencing sexual harassment in the past year. My own research demonstrates that experiences of sexual harassment and sexual assault are common among troops deployed in support of military operations in Afghanistan and Iraq, raising the possibility that servicemembers may have been exposed to multiple types of severe traumatic stress during military operations in these countries.

MST is an experience, not a diagnosis. And servicemembers and veterans will vary in their reactions to MST. Our men and women in uniform are remarkably resilient after being exposed to traumatic events, but, sadly, many will go on to face long-term difficulties with mental health after experiencing MST.

MST is strongly associated with a range of mental health conditions, but MST has a particularly strong association with PTSD. Research data from veteran samples indicates that experiences of MST are an equal or stronger predictor of PTSD, as compared to other military-related stressors, including exposure to combat.

In my clinical experience, veterans who have experienced MST often struggle with feelings of betrayal, either by perpetrators whom they believed to be comrades in arms or by the military system that they believed should have protected them. MST survivors may also struggle to integrate a victim identity with the value they place on their own strength and self-sufficiency as former or current servicemembers. Others who felt that they had to leave military service prematurely may experience grief or anger at losing a military career due to the tangible and intangible injuries caused by their alleged perpetrators, or, in their view, inadequate action taken by their leadership to protect them from such harm.

Many still think that only servicewomen experience MST, but servicemen do, too. Although the rates of sexual assault are lower among military men than among military women, in absolute numbers, more servicemen than servicewomen experienced sexual assault in the past year.

Research on the mental health consequences of sexual trauma among men has lagged behind similar research among women, but, increasingly, the data suggests that the mental health consequences of MST may be more significant for male veterans than for female veterans.

Fortunately, recovery is possible after experiences of MST. And VHA [Veterans Health Administration] has services spanning the full continuum of counseling, care, and services to assist eligible veterans in these efforts. Recognizing that many survivors of sexual trauma do not disclose their experiences unless asked directly, it is VA policy that all veterans receiving healthcare be screened for experiences of MST. Veterans who disclose MST experiences are offered a referral for mental health services. All VA counseling, care, and services determined to be necessary to overcome the psychological trauma of MST is provided free of charge. A veteran's eligibility for MST-related care is entirely separate from the veteran's entitlement to VA disability compensation for the same conditions. Every VA Medical Center provides MST-related counseling, care, and services. MST coordinators are available at every VA Medical Center to assist veterans in accessing these services.

Issues related to brain health and head trauma transcend the veteran and military community, impacting all Americans. Today, Secretary Bob McDonald is participating in VA's groundbreaking 2-day event focused on brain health, Brain Trust Pathways to Innovation. This first annual public-private partnership event is convening many of the most influential voices in the field of brain health, to include the Department of Defense, the sports industry, private sector, Federal Government, veterans, and community partners, to identify and advance solutions for mild traumatic brain injury and post-traumatic stress disorder. The event will also serve as a showcase for many of the advancements that VA is pioneering to improve brain health for veterans, the military, and for the American public.

Mr. Chairman, I appreciate the opportunity to appear before you today. And I'm prepared to answer any questions you or the committee may have.

[The prepared statement of Dr. Street follows:]

PREPARED STATEMENT BY DR. AMY STREET

Good afternoon, Chairman Graham, Ranking Member Gillibrand, and Members of the Subcommittee. Thank you for the opportunity to speak about the VA current state of research related to military sexual trauma (MST), and the diagnosis and treatment of mental health disorders associated with MST, with a particular focus on posttraumatic stress disorder (PTSD).

VA uses the term "Military Sexual Trauma" to refer to psychological trauma, which in the judgment of a mental health professional employed by the Department, results from a physical assault of a sexual nature; battery of a sexual nature; or sexual harassment, which occurred while the Veteran was serving on active duty, active duty for training, or inactive duty training. For purposes of this program, sexual harassment means repeated, unsolicited verbal or physical contact of a sexual nature which is threatening in character. MST is an experience—not a diagnosis—and Servicemembers' and Veterans' will vary in their reactions to MST. Our men and women in uniform are remarkably resilient after being exposed to traumatic events; but, sadly, many will go on to experience long-term difficulties with mental health after experiencing MST.

We know that experiences of sexual harassment and sexual assault during military service are far too common. Data from the 2014 RAND Military Workplace Study, using questionnaires that assessed incidents consistent with sex crimes under the Uniform Code of Military Justice, Article 120, indicated that 1 percent of Servicemen and 5 percent of Servicewomen were sexually assaulted in the past year, impacting an estimated 20,300 active component Servicemembers. The majority of these assaults occurred in military settings or were perpetrated by military personnel. Experiences that constitute sexual harassment are even more common. Using questionnaires that assessed incidents consistent with sex-based military equal opportunity (MEO) definitions of these offenses, seven percent of Servicemen and 22 percent of Servicewomen experienced sexual harassment in the past year. My own research demonstrates that experiences of sexual harassment and sexual assault are common among troops deployed in support of military operations in Afghanistan and Iraq, raising the possibility that Servicemembers may have been exposed to multiple types of severe traumatic stress during military operations in these countries.

Experiences of MST are strongly associated with a range of mental health conditions. These mental health disorders can include depression and substance use disorders, but experiences of MST have a particularly strong association with PTSD. In fact, research data from civilian samples demonstrates that rape is the traumatic experience with the strongest predictive probability of PTSD. Research data from Veteran samples indicates that experiences of MST are an equal or stronger predictor of PTSD as compared to other military-related stressors, including exposure to combat. In addition, experiences of MST may be a stronger predictor of PTSD than experiences of sexual assault that occurred during childhood or occur during adult civilian life. In my clinical experience, Veterans who have experienced MST often struggle with feelings of betrayal, either by perpetrators whom they believed to be "comrades in arms" or by the military system that they believe should have protected them. MST survivors may also struggle to integrate a "victim identity" with the value they place on their own strength and self-sufficiency as a former or current Servicemember. Others who felt that they had to leave military service prematurely (for instance, because of actual or perceived health or safety issues related to their MST experience) may experience grief or anger at losing a military career due to the tangible and intangible injuries caused them by their alleged perpetrators or, in their view, inadequate action taken by their leadership to protect them from such harm.

Many still think that only Servicewomen experience MST, but Servicemen do, too. Although the rates (percentages) of sexual assault are lower among military men than among military women, more Servicemen in absolute numbers than Service-women experienced sexual assaulted in the past year. Further, men who are sexu-ally assaulted are more likely than women to have been physically injured or to have been threatened with physical injury during the assault, and men's experi-ences are more likely to involve multiple assailants. Research on the mental health consequences of sexual trauma among men has lagged behind similar research among women. However, the data increasingly suggest that the associations be-tween experiences of MST and mental health disorders, while substantial for female Veterans, appear to be even stronger for male Veterans. [1]

MILITARY SEXUAL TRAUMA-RELATED CARE IN VHA

Fortunately, recovery is possible after experiences of MST, and VHA has services spanning the full continuum of counseling, care, and services to assist eligible Vet-erans in these efforts. Recognizing that many survivors of sexual trauma do not dis-close their experiences unless asked directly, it is VA policy that all Veterans receiv-ing healthcare be screened for experiences of MST. Veterans who disclose MST ex-periences are offered a referral for mental health services. All VA counseling, care, and services determined to be necessary to overcome the psychological trauma of MST, including the clinical manifestation of related PTSD, is provided free of charge. A Veteran's eligibility for MST-related counseling, care, and services is en-tirely separate from the Veteran's entitlement to VA disability compensation for the same mental health disorder(s). That is, a Veteran's eligibility for MST-related coun-seling and care is not conditioned on the Veterans Benefits Administration having adjudicated the MST-related mental health disorder to be service-connected. In ad-dition, Veterans who meet the eligibility criteria of 38 U.S.C. section 1720D(a)(1) are able to receive MST-related counseling, care, and services, even if they are not eligi-ble to be enrolled in VA's health care system or receive other VA health care. Every VA medical center provides MST-related counseling, care, and services; MST Coordi-nators are available at every VA medical center to assist Veterans in accessing these services. Many community-based Vet Centers also have specially-trained MST counselors.

EFFECTIVE TREATMENT OF PTSD

VA is strongly committed to delivering quality care to all Veterans with PTSD, including those whose PTSD results from MST. Advances in research have led to a range of effective treatments for PTSD that reduce symptoms and increase func-tioning and well-being. The VA/DOD Clinical Practice Guidelines, titled *Manage-ment of Post-Traumatic Stress Disorder and Acute Stress Reaction* (2010)), rec-ommend trauma-focused cognitive behavioral therapy [such as Prolonged Exposure (PE), and Cognitive Processing Therapy (CPT)], Eye Movement Desensitization and Reprocessing, stress inoculation, selective serotonin reuptake inhibitors, and venlafaxine, a serotonin norepinephrine reuptake inhibitor, as primary treatments for PTSD. PE and CPT are among the most widely studied types of trauma-focused cognitive behavioral therapy. Evidence demonstrating their effectiveness is particu-larly strong. These treatments have great relevance for MST survivors as much of the early work developing and testing both PE and CPT occurred among sexual as-sault survivors in the civilian population.

VHA Handbook 1160.01, *Uniform Mental Health Services in VA Medical Centers and Clinics,* requires that all VA medical centers provide access to either PE or CPT. VA has supported this requirement by training upwards of 7,000 therapists in these treatments as part of a broader initiative to disseminate evidence-based psychotherapy for mental health disorders. Uptake of PE and CPT across the VA health care system was rapid; by 2009, 96 percent of VA facilities were providing PE or CPT and 72 percent were providing both. VA also offers a range of treatment options to treat PTSD and associated symptoms and is using telehealth technologies to increase the availability of treatment for PTSD. VA remains open to new and in-

[1] Gender differences in experiences of sexual harassment: data from a male-dominated envi-ronment.
AE Street, JL Gradus, J Stafford, K Kelly—Journal of consulting and clinical psychology, 2007
Ann Epidemiol. 2005 Mar;15(3):191–5.
The role of sexual assault on the risk of PTSD among Gulf War Veterans.
Kang H [1], Dalager N, Mahan C, Ishii E.
J Trauma Stress. 2005 Jun;18(3):272–84.
Deployment stressors, gender, and mental health outcomes among Gulf War I Veterans.
Vogt DS[1], Pless AP, King LA, King DW.

novative treatments for PTSD and supports research on these treatments as part of its portfolio on PTSD and related mental health disorders.

CONCLUSION

Mr. Chairman, I appreciate the opportunity to appear before you today. I am prepared to answer any questions you or other Members of the Committee may have.

Senator GRAHAM. Well, thank you all very much.

I'll start. And it was a excellent——

Dr. Street, if someone is a victim of sexual assault in the military, can they get a disability rating because of the PTS [Post-traumatic Stress]?

Dr. STREET. So, a disability rating would be provided for PTSD. So, because military sexual trauma is the experience and not the diagnosis, it would be the diagnosis related to the experience—in this case, PTSD—that the disability rating would come from. And yes, they can.

Senator GRAHAM. So, if someone has been assaulted, and they get PTSD, they qualify.

Dr. STREET. That's right. They would then go through the same process that a veteran who experienced PTSD related to com- bat——

Senator GRAHAM. Okay.

Dr. STREET.—that same disability assessment process.

Senator GRAHAM. Captain Greenhalgh, when—what's the process we use when people return from the battle theater, in terms of evaluating them to make sure that we're catching things that they may have experienced?

Captain GREENHALGH. Yes, sir. Well, the—you know, if we're talking about traumatic brain injury, for example, it actually doesn't start after they leave the battlefield; it starts on the battlefield, with—not necessarily symptom-related evaluations and screening, but event-related. So, if a servicemember, for example, is involved in a—an IED [improvised explosive device]—if they're within 50 meters of an IED blast, for example, or a rollover accident, it's not up to, necessarily, the medical leadership to say they need to get screened; the line leadership, the battle buddy, will ensure that that person is screened on the battlefield or at the local, you know, forward medical unit. So, that's when the screening does begin.

Now, certainly if somebody falls through that crack or is not, you know, involved in a significant——

Senator GRAHAM. Right.

Captain GREENHALGH.—injury or event, when they return from the battlefield, there is immediate post-deployment health risk assessments that are performed. Actually, a cycle of three of them are performed within—shortly after return, then 90 days later, 180 days later.

Senator GRAHAM. What have we—how old is this system?

Captain GREENHALGH. Excuse me, sir?

Senator GRAHAM. How old is this system that you've just described?

Captain GREENHALGH. Well, I, myself, deployed about 4 years ago, and it had already been in effect several years before that. Now, it's been modified, I think, you know, at——

Senator GRAHAM. Do you think it's working?

Captain GREENHALGH. I think it's as good as it can be right now, because we are—you know, we're basically not waiting for the patients to come to us with——

Senator GRAHAM. Right.

Captain GREENHALGH.—symptoms; we're basically asking them about symptoms that maybe others wouldn't necessarily associate with a traumatic brain injury, and they're——

Senator GRAHAM. When it comes to prevention—I'm sure there are all kind of technical things we're trying to do to protect the brain in a IED attack, but when it comes to PTS or—what kind of preventive measures are we employing?

Captain GREENHALGH. With regards to the psychological health, sir?

Senator GRAHAM. Yes.

Captain GREENHALGH. I mean, I think that prevention begins long before they deploy, and it has to do with training and—being adequately trained and knowing their—you know, kind of knowing their algorithms. You know, we don't want to overtrain people. You want—you know, when they're in training, you would say, you know, "train like you fight," but you want them to have adequate rest, let—to allow, you know, brain rest, as well. But, you know, sort of——

Senator GRAHAM. Are we teaching people what to watch out for in their buddies?

Captain GREENHALGH. No, absolutely. I think there's—just from the psychological health perspective, certainly, and from the traumatic brain injury perspective, as well, there's a lot of training that goes on before they deploy. And then, depending on how long a servicemember is in theater, there's mandatory screening that occurs if they're there for more than 6 months, even if they're not involved in any sort of any specific event.

Senator GRAHAM. Do you feel you have adequate resources at the moment to do your job?

Captain GREENHALGH. Well, sir, you know, we'd always love to have more.

Senator GRAHAM. Right.

Captain GREENHALGH. But, I think that, especially with a drawdown in commitments overseas, what we're finding is that the resources aren't necessarily needed for the Active, you know, returning-off-the-battlefield servicemember as much as they were just 3 or 4 years ago. I think it's more for the long-term commitment that we have to these servicemembers, some of whom were injured years ago, understanding that it's not a, you know, patch 'em up and send 'em back out to the real world. Some of these——

Senator GRAHAM. Right.

Captain GREENHALGH.—people suffer for years. And along with our, you know, VA colleagues, this is a long-term commitment, and that's where I think the nature of the type of support that we need definitely changes.

Senator GRAHAM. Do you think the handoff between DOD and the VA is working?

Captain GREENHALGH. I think it's working better than it ever has, sir.

14

Senator GRAHAM. Do you agree with that, Ms. Street—Dr. Street?

Dr. STREET. I do.

Senator GRAHAM. Captain Colston, you said that 25 percent of the force has been treated for—for what?

Captain COLSTON. Yes, sir. So, one of the things that we actually do is, in transition, where we—when we do handoffs from DOD to VA, we look at who's been treated in the last year. And it's at about 20 percent for psychological health conditions, and then, for other conditions, such as substance-use disorders, pain disorders, depression, that kicks it over 25 percent. So, we have a large cohort of treated people right now, sir.

Senator GRAHAM. So, from a DOD perspective, this is a problem.

Captain COLSTON. Oh, absolutely, sir. And it's one, certainly, that we've devoted a lot of resources to, that we have really made a number of turnarounds for.

Senator GRAHAM. Well, just to stay within time, here—do you see any promising therapies in the future? Hyperbaric oxygen treatment, I've heard a lot about that. There's a program, I think, in Myrtle Beach. People really believe in it. There are all kind of ideas out there. Could you tell me a little bit about that treatment and what you see coming in the future?

Captain COLSTON. Well, I think hyperbaric oxygen treatment, we've done about seven studies on that right now. None of them failed to show any effect beyond a placebo effect. But, we have all kinds of innovative strategies, and we also have a number of A-level evidence-based strategies for PTSD. I think innovations in the future are going to include biomarkers, neuroimaging, and, really, better ascertainment of the disease states of PTSD and TBI and the other things that run with it.

Senator GRAHAM. Okay. Well, we'll let the hyperbaric people—you'll have your say. You can write us a report about it.

Senator Gillibrand.

Senator GILLIBRAND. Thank you, Mr. Chairman.

Victims and experts have stated that the response to military sexual trauma is more similar to that of incest than other forms of sexual assault. How many survivors of MST go on to develop PTSD, is the first question? And for MST survivors who develop PTSD, how do they present differently from those with PTSD stemming from other kinds of traumatic events?

Doctor?

Dr. STREET. We know that experiences of sexual assault, including experiences of sexual assault during military service, are one of the strongest predictors of PTSD. It's the type of event that's associated with PTSD symptoms among both women and men, as I mentioned, even more strongly for men than for women.

And the symptoms of PTSD related to MST look really quite similar than the symptoms of PTSD related to other forms of traumatic stress, although survivors of MST may report certain kinds of issues more frequently than other types of trauma survivors. So, for example, issues around intimacy and sexuality, issues around interpersonal relationships and boundaries, certainly issues around trust, issues around self-blame. Those are issues that come up, I think, much more frequently in—when working with sexual trauma survivors.

Senator GILLIBRAND. In the last report we got, 62 percent of the people who reported that they were sexually assaulted were retaliated against—from their perspective, some form of retaliation. How does the experience of not being believed or being retaliated against affect PTSD symptoms?

Dr. STREET. It worsens it. I've done research indicating that a victim's experiences in reporting, in the system, and how they feel about that experience—if they feel positively about it, if they feel like they were believed—that is a strong predictor above and beyond the traumatic experience of how they're doing, years later, in terms of PTSD and depression symptoms.

Senator GILLIBRAND. Last December, there was a study completed by the VA researchers that was published in the American Journal of Preventive Medicine on the link between military sexual trauma and death by suicide. The study found that MST was a significant risk factor for suicide among men and women, even controlling for other psychiatric disorders. What implications do these findings have for screening and treating patients with MST?

And then, to Captain Colston, how do these findings inform screenings and treatment of servicemembers? And what kind of outreach do you encourage survivors of MST to seek care?

Dr. STREET. So, we do, as I mentioned, screen every veteran for experiences of MST, in the VA, which that study would suggest is particularly important, because, unlike other types of traumatic events, the risk associated with MST for suicide doesn't run fully through PTSD or depression; it exists separate from that. So, it's just why it's so important that we screen specifically for experiences of military sexual trauma, so that those patients can be followed up with, in terms of suicide risk, directly.

Senator GILLIBRAND. Captain?

Captain COLSTON. Yes, ma'am. I'd agree with—yes, ma'am, I'd agree with Dr. Street. Suicide risk is increased from sexual assaults, aside from PTSD. PTSD itself is not necessarily a robust risk factor for suicide. It does have a hazard ratio that suggests that it's associated with suicide, but certainly sexual trauma is a really big factor.

Developmental trauma, especially developmental sexual trauma, stuff that I've seen as a child psychiatrist, that's a huge risk factor and something that actually affects the brain as it develops, makes you kind of check the horizon for if you're safe all the time.

Senator GILLIBRAND. Although the prevalence for military sexual trauma is higher among women, given the significantly larger portion of men in the Armed Forces, there are similar numbers of men and women who have survived sexual trauma. How do men differ in their response to MST? And how do VA services meet the unique needs of men who have survived MST? And are treatments for PTSD related to MST different for men and women? And, if so, how? And is there a detectable difference in male suicide rates?

Dr. STREET. So, male and female survivors of MST look more similar than they do different, although men's experiences may be exacerbated, in terms of symptomatology, although the symptoms themselves are the same. Men—male survivors do struggle uniquely with concerns about their masculinity, understanding what this says about their sexual orientation, a lot of self-blame, "Why was I targeted for this?" This isn't something that men usually experience.

In terms of treatments, the treatments look very similar. I think differences, in terms of male and female survivors, really comes in when we think about our social marketing and our outreach. We're very careful to have outreach materials that are specifically targeted to male survivors, to include pictures of men on all of our outreach materials about MST, in addition to pictures of women, so that men can understand that our MST treatment services are there for them as well as those for women.

Captain COLSTON. I'd say one of the things that we struggle with, the prevalence of sexual assault in women compared to men is probably about five to one. And Dr. Street's data and Nate Galbreath's data at SAPRO, and some of Ron Kessler's data from Harvard, support that.

One of the things that we struggle with is getting men into care. Men are less apt to engage in care for sexual assault. And, in fact, in therapy, that's something that you may address way downstream. It's not an initial or presenting problem.

Senator GILLIBRAND. It's why I have a concern that the suicide rate might be higher, because if——

Captain COLSTON. Well, I——

Senator GILLIBRAND.—male survivors won't report, they don't get any care. And, just anecdotally, I met a male survivor who attempted suicide, was not successful, paralyzed himself in his— shooting himself in the spine, and was paralyzed for the rest of his life. But, he couldn't face his life, he couldn't face his wife, he couldn't face anything after it. And instead of seeking treatment— or, actually—he actually did, but, for many survivors, instead of seeking treatment, they just commit suicide.

Captain COLSTON. There's no question that it's a trauma that's very hard to overcome. And it's very hard for us to get granular exactly about what the problem is. There's——

Senator GILLIBRAND. Yeah.

Captain COLSTON.—on the order of 300 risk factors associated with suicide. Certainly, sexual assault is one of them. PTSD is one of them.

One thing is, I think, you know, with regard to VA care and some of the promising things, we see that veterans who have PTSD have lower suicide rates than other veterans. So, I think there are some promising developments in the treatment and in the turnover from DOD to VA.

Senator GILLIBRAND. Thank you.

Senator GRAHAM. For the record, Senator Cotton served a tour of duty in combat in Iraq. I think you were a platoon leader and— is that correct?

So, Senator Cotton.

Senator COTTON. Thank you, Chairman Graham.

And I can say that the system that Captain Greenhalgh described has been in effect for at least 10 years, at least in the Army.

I want to talk briefly about the relationship between traumatic
brain injury and post-traumatic stress. Does—one does not necessarily presume or infer the other. Is that correct?

Captain GREENHALGH. Not necessarily, sir. I think, certainly, if
someone has been exposed in a traumatic event downrange that resulted in a traumatic brain injury, I think the possibility is greater
that they will also have comorbid post-traumatic stress along with
that. I do believe that a history of TBI sort of predisposes someone
to be more vulnerable to psychological health issues downrange, or
down the road. And some of that has to do with the chronic effects,
if that is a servicemember who has chronic effects of the TBI, developing some symptoms that are very suggestive also of psychological health issues. There's a lot of overlap there, as well.

Captain COLSTON. And I'd say patients often present to us in an
undifferentiated state. They'll present, maybe, with their—with a
problem with suicidality, maybe a substance-use disorder, maybe a
pain disorder. Sometimes it's very hard for us to discern what the
precipitant was.

Dr. STREET. I have nothing to add.

Senator COTTON. Is one easier to diagnose than the other?

Captain GREENHALGH. From a——

Senator COTTON. To the extent that you can separate the comorbidity of the two.

Captain GREENHALGH. Well—so, my background, sir, is primary
care, so I would say, certainly, we see a lot of behavioral health in
the primary care setting. But, given that, we have very strong
CPGs for a lot of things that we take care of in the—you know, in
military medicine and just medicine in general.

When I see a patient who has a history that sort of fits within
the clinical practice guideline description for certain kind of diagnosis, I find that, from the primary care perspective, the TBI is certainly an easy one to try and fit into that, you know, diagnostic
realm.

Captain COLSTON. Some of it has to do with the patients that
present in front of us. For Walt, in a primary care setting, he's
going to see a different patient population than I'll see in a psychiatric setting. One of the things that occurs to me is, the science
for PTSD is probably more developed than the science is for TBI.
Science for TBI is really in a nascent stage, so PTSD is a little easier to discern. It's a little easier to discern from a child psychiatry
standpoint with regard to developmental trauma, just because the
prevalence of that is so high.

Dr. STREET. And just to add, I concur that the research base on
PTSD is a bit further along. And, as part of that, we have existing
well-validated instruments for the screening and diagnosis of
PTSD. And I think those instruments are being developed for TBI,
but are not as far along, haven't undergone as rigorous tests.

Captain GREENHALGH. If I——

Senator COTTON. So, the science for PTS is further along than
TBI. Is that simply because of the volume of patients that the medical world has seen with post-traumatic stress, as opposed to TBI?

Captain COLSTON. I think it's a number of factors. The science of
TBI is—has been really hard to get a handle on, just from the
standpoint of—you know, it took—I'll give you an example, sir—it

18

took 20 years and $50 billion to get on top of HIV [Human Immunodeficiency Virus]. HIV has about a dozen genes and two serotypes. The brain uses about 20,000 of the 30,000 genes in the human genome. Understanding the way the brain works, especially a brain that's traumatized, is extremely hard.

With regard to PTSD, we at least have a long history of looking at people who were traumatized, and a long history of treatment interventions, so I think the science is more developed for that reason. The prevalences of both of those—in DOD, the prevalence of TB—of PTSD is about 2 percent; TBI, slightly lower.

Dr. STREET. I think, from a historical perspective, we really became aware of PTSD, following the Vietnam War. And so, we've had that span of history to really think about the disorder, the diagnosis, and the treatment of the disorder. TBI is something that we've become so much more aware of, due to the recent conflicts in Iraq and Afghanistan.

Captain GREENHALGH. And, if I could just add, sir. Again, from the primary care perspective, there have been versions of PTS, it seems, from conflicts centuries ago, as well, this—the idea of shell-shock and things like that. I think we've gotten more of a handle on it after the Vietnam conflict. But, as Captain Colston alluded to, with technology, neuroimaging capacity, that really has just been a phenomenon of our generation. And so, I think there's a lot of potential there. And again, from the primary care perspective, having neuroimaging support certain diagnostic criteria for traumatic brain injury, I think that's where there's a lot of potential for the science. But, I agree, I think we've been describing things like PTS for quite a lot longer than we have traumatic brain injury.

Senator COTTON. One word I think I heard you use twice, maybe three times, was "longitudinal." The root of that is "long," which is a little worsened, given the number of people who suffer from PTS or TBI. Obviously, when you're conducting a longitudinal study, it takes many years to get results. Is that something about which we should be concerned?

Captain COLSTON. Yes, sir, but it's the only way that we can do it, because these things don't present in silos. PTS doesn't present in a silo. TBI doesn't present in a silo. So, we've got to get a handle on where the patients are. And we have a lot of efforts. We've got the millennium cohort study, we've got the 15-year TBI study. We have the STARRS [Study to Assess Risk and Resilience in Servicemembers] longitudinal study on suicide. So, we're looking at several hundred-thousand patients now to get an idea of where patients are coming from.

Captain GREENHALGH. And if I can add onto that, "longitudinal" doesn't mean that we have to wait until the study is over to start gathering data, so the 15-year study, for example, has report-outs every 4 years. The next one is due next year. Not to mention the constant stream of data and research that is being formulated into papers and publications along the way. That's just a small example.

So, longitudinal really, I think, if anything, connotes a commitment to a long-term study of this, not to say that we're going to not give you any answers for 15 more years, sir.

Senator COTTON. Can—do you, can you, would it be productive to expand the dataset to look at other occupations that might have similar risk factors, like, say, professional football, professional hockey, boxing? There may be others.

Dr. STREET. Certainly, the brain trust meeting that I described that's happening today and tomorrow is doing exactly that, and it's bringing in a researcher from my institution who was one of the first to identify this issue among professional football players, and taking that information and then applying it to the military and veteran community. So, for sure, these public-private partnerships in which you can identify knowledge that's been gathered in other places and applied to this population, I think are very promising.

Senator GRAHAM. Senator Blumenthal.

Senator BLUMENTHAL. Thanks, Mr. Chairman.

Dr. Street, I think you've touched briefly on the transition from Active Duty out of service or into the Reserves or care of the Veterans Administration. How well do you think that transition is going these days, in terms of the computer compatibility, not only in records, but also in transition on pharmaceutical drugs, the prescriptions, and so forth? Maybe you can give us an overview, because I think you're—you really are in a position to comment on that issue.

Dr. STREET. Well, I'm happy to comment from my perspective, although my perspective may be a bit limited, so you may choose to hear from my colleagues, as well. But, in my perspective as a practicing clinician, that transition is going well. I think Captain Greenhalgh, earlier, said it's going better than it ever has. And I know that there's a lot of attention to this issue, a lot of new initiatives. And, in my experience as a practicing clinician, I haven't encountered problems with that.

Captain COLSTON. Sir, I'd say it's DOD policy right now that we do a warm handoff from DOD to VA. And it's really important, those transitions. One of the things that we've done is, we've established coaching, an in-transition program, where we actually look at people's medical data and then go in and say, "Hey, can we help you with your follow-on appointments?" And I think that's been used to good effect in the last year.

Senator BLUMENTHAL. Well, it's always been the policy. It's not always been the executed policy. And so, for example, on the interoperability of computer programs, I don't know whether you can give us an up-to-date perspective on how well that's going. It's been a continuing struggle, as you know.

Dr. STREET. I don't have an update on the status of that. I'm—but, I'm happy to take that question for the record, and we could get back to you with a more thorough answer on the updated status of that integration process.

Senator BLUMENTHAL. I would appreciate that. And, as well, on the pharmaceutical drug issue, the transition there has been an issue for some time.

Senator BLUMENTHAL. Let me shift to, again, the post-traumatic stress, military sexual assault trauma. Is that an area where you think more research, as well as clinical treatment, is necessary?

Dr. STREET. I'm a researcher. I'll always say that I think more research is necessary. But, I do think this is a case where under-

standing things that are unique about experiences of military sexual assault, ways in which those experiences differ when they're in
the military context from when they're in a civilian context, and
better understanding that has a lot of implications for recovery. So,
I think our—research that helps us understand that process, as
well as research more generally targeted to the disorder and treatment of the disorder, is extremely valuable.

Senator BLUMENTHAL. And it may seem obvious—the answer
may seem obvious. I think I have an idea about what the answer
is, but maybe you can talk a little bit about what the differences
are in the civilian-versus-military sexual assault trauma.

Dr. STREET. Sure. Senator Gillibrand, earlier, referred to the fact
that survivors of military sexual assault in some ways looked clinically more like survivors of childhood sexual abuse than they look
like survivors of adult sexual assault in the civilian world. And I
think there's some truth to that, certainly in terms of the fact that
survivors from military sexual trauma often talk about the experience of ongoing abuse in which they feel trapped and unable to es-
cape because they're not able to, sort of, leave their position, although there have been policy improvements to make that more
possible. They're also dependent, often, on their perpetrators for
meeting their basic health needs or for this feeling that their perpetrators are those who are supposed to be watching their back
and looking out for them. And I think those kinds of differences
gives the survivor, sometimes, a little bit of a flavor for—that looks
more like ongoing childhood abuse.

Of course, also, we know that survivors of traumatic stress are
often repeatedly traumatized over a lifespan. So, that earlier trauma increases risk for later trauma. So, many women and men who
are survivors of sexual trauma in the military are also survivors
of childhood sexual trauma or other interpersonal trauma, as well.
So, then those experiences can exacerbate each other, in terms of
the severity of the symptom presentation.

Senator BLUMENTHAL. Thank you.

My time is expired. But, I appreciate your taking my earlier
questions for the record. Thank you very much.

And thank you all for your service.

Thank you.

Senator GRAHAM. Thank you. I think Senator Tillis is on the
way, but I—Senator Gillibrand, if you have any follow-up.

Senator GILLIBRAND. One of the issues that some of us work on
is rescheduling marijuana to become a Schedule 2 drug so more research can be done and so patients that have been prescribed the
medication can get access to it more regularly. One of the concerns
we've had is, because it's a Schedule 1 drug, it, therefore, prohibits
the VA from being able to prescribe it, even though that individual
might have been prescribed in their State, where their State's already passed a law. We've heard, anecdotally, from many veterans
that marijuana can often be a very useful treatment for PTSD
symptoms. Have you studied that issue? Do you have any insight
into that issue that you'd like to share?

Captain COLSTON. Ma'am, I can say DOD hasn't ascertained the
answer to that question, for the reason that you——

Senator GILLIBRAND. For the Schedule 1.

Captain COLSTON.—just asked earlier.

One thing that I have seen, as a child psychiatrist, is, there's risks and benefits to any intervention. And with regard to marijuana, one of the things that we struggle with is, it can precipitate psychosis in some people, especially younger people, people of a military age. So, that would be a concern that I would have as we press forward on this.

Dr. STREET. I know that VA has ongoing studies looking at the effectiveness of marijuana for a treatment of PTSD, but I know that there have been issues that have come up related to the quality of the marijuana, the consistency of the marijuana, the strength of the marijuana, that's made it—there are unique challenges, in terms of studying the effectiveness of that substance on the disorder.

Senator GILLIBRAND. Would you recommend further study of it so that we could actually have drug companies study it and drug companies produce medicines that then can be tested?

Dr. STREET. I'd like to see the results of the early studies, in terms of addressing the, sort of, cost-benefit analysis. If early studies looked promising, then I would make that recommendation. But, if early studies showed a lot of negotiate, unexpected effects, then I would be more cautious in that recommendation.

Senator GILLIBRAND. Thank you.

Senator GRAHAM. Senator Sullivan.

Senator SULLIVAN. Thank you, Mr. Chair. And I appreciate you and the Ranking Member calling this hearing. It's a very important topic.

You know, appreciate the witnesses being here. One of the things I really like about this committee, it's very bipartisan. And this topic comes up a lot in a very bipartisan way. You see members who actually really, really care about this. I certainly happen to be one of them. I think most people who have served in the military can recall more than one instances where a troop member of their squad or unit or—has succumbed to the—to depression and suicide. And I think it—it's a searing experience, of course, for families, but for the troops and the leadership and everybody else who goes through that. So, it's a topic that we need to do a better job at.

I'm sure that's probably already been covered to some degree, but—What authorities would you view, from our perspective, that you need from this committee or the Congress to do more to address some of the issues of the stigma PTSD or reducing the rates of suicide among our Active Duty and veteran populations? Is there anything more you need from us?

Captain GREENHALGH. Well, sir, I think you talk about two things that are very closely related, which is reducing the rate—reducing the stigma and then attacking the problem, itself, which is suicide. And I think, with regards to reducing the stigma, we've made great strides over the last decade, I think, at least, in making it not just a, again, symptom-drive approach, the patient coming to the medical provider, looking for help. With our screening efforts, certainly everybody is asked whether they're symptomatic or not. When we go through our annual health maintenance examinations, that comes up as a very prominent topic, that and TBI history, as well as a lot of the technology and, sort of, the apps that are avail-

able, a lot of, you know, IT solutions, where the servicemember
doesn't—and their family—doesn't necessarily have to go to a clinician to ask the question. They can get a lot of the information they
need online. And I think that goes a long way towards
destigmatizing, if they can at least get the answer to some of their
preliminary questions in, sort of, a non-sort-of-clinical environment.
I think that's certainly one step.

Captain Colston?

Captain COLSTON. With regard to resources, I wouldn't necessarily have anything to say about that. I would say that there
is a robust relationship between suicide and depression. And certainly identification and management of depression, especially in a
primary care setting, is a very important strategy, and one that we
really want to focus on, really in public health.

Senator SULLIVAN. Let me ask another question that relates to,
kind of, my first one on authorities. There is a bill—and I'm having
my team take a look at it—that I've been looking at. I believe it
might be Senator Peters who has put this bill forward, that—and
I don't want to butcher it here, so we can make sure you get it for
the record—but that is concerned about claims that there's been
thousands, maybe tens of thousands, of members of the military
who have received discharges that are less-than-honorable discharges related to PTSD or brain-injury type of issues. And are you
familiar with this bill, or are you familiar with—and the bill would
ask the military to have a presumption, maybe, in favor of a honorable discharge. In my military career, have not really seen that
issue, but I may have been missing something. Are you familiar
with this bill? Are you familiar with the problem? And what's your
advice? Do you think there's thousands, or even more, members of
the military who have been discharged with other-than-honorable
designation because of activities of undiagnosed PTSD, and that
their discharge designation should be relooked at? And do you need
authority to do that, from the Congress?

Captain COLSTON. Sir, on the bright side, we've already had that
authority, and we've used it. So, we've—we did a mental health review, where we looked at over 200,000 boards. We did a physical
disability board review, where we looked at a number of boards for
just that problem. And since 2007, patients that you are going to
separate for means, be they disciplinary, be they for lack of performance, they need to be—PTSD issues and TBI issues need to be
addressed before that can be done.

And when we look at the numbers, we look at—we used to separate about 4,000 folks a year for personality disorder separations.
That number is down to 300. So, that number is about 7 percent
of what it was. There's been a lot of attention to this issue. And
certainly—about 3 years ago, I think we spent on the order of $10
million looking at boards. And certainly, as Senator Blumenthal's
brought up in some previous correspondence with DOD, sometimes
we're going all the way back, so the boards of correction for military records have looked at cases from Vietnam veterans, cases
even where PTSD didn't exist as a clinical diagnosis. Of course, it's
hard to ascertain, you know, exactly what the circumstances were
around something that happened a long time ago without records.

Senator SULLIVAN. So, you——

Sorry, Mr. Chairman. Just a follow-up.

If you—so, you already have that authority. Have you seen this bill? And have you weighed in on it? And—it would be very useful. It's, like I said, something that I've—I'm very sympathetic to. I don't know what DOD thinks about the bill. At the same time, it sounds like you're already—you already have the authority to do what the bill does. I don't know if it has a presumption in favor of a honorable discharge or—again, I don't know the specifics. I'm sorry, I should have brought it with me. But, have you weighed in, or do you need the authorities, or you think you're good to go in addressing this—what you're obviously saying is a problem?

Captain GREENHALGH. Well, sir, I mean, I haven't seen the bill. I haven't been asked to weigh in. But, I echo what Captain Colston said, is that I don't think it's an issue of the type of discharge that a patient gets. I think it's a matter of ensuring that they get the correct kind of care that they need prior to discharge, or even after discharge, with that warm handoff to our VA colleagues. Whether it's honorable or dishonorable, I think, is—isn't necessarily the driving point.

Senator SULLIVAN. Mr. Chairman, if I may, maybe we can submit that bill. And if they had a view on it——

Senator GRAHAM. Yeah. Well, it sort of is the driving point, because you don't want someone to have a UOTHC, other-than-honorable-conditions discharge, who had a medical condition that may have resulted in it.

Senator SULLIVAN. Right.

Senator GRAHAM. That's the whole point.

Dr. STREET. And this was particularly relevant or military sexual trauma survivors. They were often diagnosed with a personality disorder as part of their discharge after they had suffered a sexual assault. And with that discharge, they weren't entitled to VA benefits. So, it was a huge problem for them——

Senator GRAHAM. Yeah.

Dr. STREET.—because they have trauma, they've been—they're a survivor, they need mental health care, and they don't even have access to the VA anymore. So, that—we wanted those cases to be looked at again to say, Can we get this right?

Senator GRAHAM. Yeah, we—we'll upgrade the discharge if there's a medical reason that was missed, or PTS suffering.

Captain Colston, the reviews you're familiar with, did you all actually change discharge designations?

Captain COLSTON. Yes, sir. So, several servicemembers have had discharge determinations changed over the years. And several servicemembers have had their benefits changed. So, especially the Physical Disability Board of Review——

Senator GRAHAM. Could you do this? Could you have that group—and I applaud your efforts—give us the results? I mean— of the 200,000 reviewed, how many discharges were upgraded and how many benefits were restored?

Captain COLSTON. Yes, sir. The executive agent for that was the Air Force and the Physical Disability Board of Review is right here——

Senator GRAHAM. Our crack staff——

Captain COLSTON.—inside the Beltway.

Senator GRAHAM.—will get on that, won't you, crack staff? Absolutely.

Senator King.

Senator KING. Thank you, Mr. Chairman.

[The information referred to follows:]

DOD has undertaken three coordinated efforts to upgrade discharge characterizations, dating back to the Vietnam-era, from other than honorable characterizations, change administrative separations to military retirements, and otherwise scrub all disability boards started under a mental health claim since 2001, for a potential increase in benefits. These efforts are carried out by the Boards of Correction for Military Records (BCMRs).

The results that you are inquiring about were from the review initiated in October 2012, by order of the then-Secretary of Defense, Leon Panetta, requiring the existing Physical Disability Board of Review (PDBR) to conduct a comprehensive review of mental health diagnoses from September 11, 2001 to April 30, 2012, for Service members who completed a disability evaluation process and whose mental health diagnoses were changed during that process. The PDBR completed a review of 200,000 cases where a disability board was started and then changed or stopped, for reasons such as change in diagnoses of post-traumatic stress disorder (PTSD), adjustment disorders, depression, anxiety or possible removal of diagnoses stemming from other factors, such as disciplinary proceedings. This effort was undertaken to audit the system in an analytically sound, non-bureaucratic, and action-oriented manner to mitigate the risk of bias toward diverting Service members away from compensable disabilities.

No evidence of bias was found. Of the 200,000 cases processed by the Services for eligibility, about 5 percent (11,000) were found eligible for reconsideration using a permissive administrative filter. All eligible individuals received at least two, and most times three, mailings, with return receipts requested, that invited them to apply to the PDBR for consideration for changes to the military record. About 1000 were returned by applicants. 100 of the cases either met the eligibility criteria for consideration (66 cases resulting in 10 medical retirements) or contained other discrepancies that accrued to the benefit of the applicants (34 cases). Those 34 cases, processed under the rationale that the PDBR application was nested within a Boards of Correction for Military Review (BCMR) application, resulted in 7 additional findings for medical retirements by the BCMRs.

Subsequent to the above review, then-Secretary of Defense Chuck Hagel, issued a memorandum focused upon the petitions of Vietnam veterans to Military Department Boards for Correction of Military/Naval Records for the purpose of upgrading their discharges based on claims of previously unrecognized PTSD, as PTSD was not yet recognized as a diagnosis during this period of history. Thirty-eight percent of Vietnam-era petitioners have been granted relief, a figure that is significantly higher than that for standard discharge upgrade requests. The latest numbers indicate the Department has received 759 qualifying petitions, 273 of which have been adjudicated and 486 of which are still pending resolution. Of those that have been adjudicated, 103 were granted upgrades.

Another effort currently underway by the DOD's Physical Disability Board of Review (PDBR), is looking at 77,000 medical boards where combined disability ratings of 20 percent or less were assigned to Service members who were discharged between September 11, 2001 and December 31, 2009. Many of these cases stemmed from decrements in disability findings stemming from existence of non-compensable mental health conditions, such as personality disorders or adjustment disorders. In almost 25 percent of the cases reviewed by the PDBR, an applicant became eligible for a disability retirement. Members who prevailed in this forum were awarded monthly disability retirement pay and TRICARE eligibility for themselves and eligible dependents retroactive to the day of original disability separation.

To ensure that mental health conditions are rightfully considered, the DOD has implemented section 521 of the Carl Levin and Howard P. "Buck" McKeon National Defense Authorization Act for Fiscal Year 2015, P .L. 113–291, by: 1) including the opinion of a clinical psychologist or psychiatrist if the review for correction of records includes a mental health disorder; and 2) including on the board a clinical psychologist, psychiatrist, or physician with training on mental health issues pertaining to post-traumatic stress disorder (PTSD) and traumatic brain injury (TBI) when there is a request for review by a Service member diagnosed with PTSD or TBI while deployed or with a mental health disorder while serving in the military.

Thank you all for your work in what is a really important area. We see it daily in Maine.

Dr. Street, one of the issues we have in our State—it's a very rural State, it's large—large, long distances. How do we deal with the unique challenges facing veterans in PTSD and other mental issues who—it's just almost impossible to drive a whole day, and drive back, and to have effective treatment. Talk to me about treat- ing this problem in rural areas, and particularly about the possi- bility of using online resources, telemedicine, those kinds of things. Dr. STREET. Well, you're—the things you suggest are exactly the kinds of things that we've been working with, really figuring out how we can harness technology to take what we know are effective treatments, but have used—been, historically, in a sort of face-to- face setting in an office situation, and use technology to make those more widely available. So, certainly telehealth. But, increasingly now, we've also been developing and testing online technologies. So, for an example, a colleague of mine in Boston recently developed a online intervention for comorbid PTSD and alcohol abuse that's— that, in early stages, is showing—shown to be quite effective. We are also harnessing the use of mobile apps that veterans can use, if they have infrequent appointments, in between appointments to help manage their symptoms and improve their process of recovery. So, we're hoping that use of technologies, and really harnessing those technologies, can help address some of the issues with treat- ment among rural veterans.

Senator KING. Just as sort of a parenthetical question, then I'll get back to the technology. Do we know what works? Is—are there proven treatments to deal with this issue?

Dr. STREET. There are. And it's, I think, such an important mes- sage to get out there. So—because I think it provides hope for vet- erans. But, we have well-established, rigorously-tested treatments for PTSD, primarily psychotherapies in the cognitive behavioral realm that have been shown, in multiple settings, in multiple popu- lations, to be very effective in reducing the incidence of PTSD.

Senator KING. I think that's important news out of this hear- ing——

Dr. STREET. Absolutely.

Senator KING.—that this is not a hopeless situation, that there are——

Dr. STREET. Absolutely.

Senator KING.—successful treatments.

Dr. STREET. Absolutely.

Senator KING. Well, I want to encourage you, in the strongest possible terms, to pursue these technological advances, because time is not on our side. And again, in many places in this country, people are in very rural areas—in Alaska—and they just don't— they just don't have access to a clinic or to a group. It's very dif- ficult.

Dr. Colston, talk—let's talk about substance abuse as it relates to this issue. Do you—I'm—from my anecdotal data from my staff in Maine, there's a lot of overlap. A lot of people that have PTSD end up in a substance-abuse situation, either alcohol or drugs. Is that true? And how do we deal with that issue?

Captain COLSTON. Yes, sir. There's about a 30-percent overlap between PTSD and substance-use disorders. And one of the really scary things that we're facing right now is the scourge of opiate overdose deaths in this country. So, as people transition——

Senator KING. 47,000 a year.

Captain COLSTON. Yes, sir. Just horrible. And certainly, as people have transitioned into heroin use, more heroin overdoses——

Senator KING. Do you think part of it is self-medication?

Captain COLSTON. Yes, sir, no question. And we've seen that with alcohol. We've seen it with all kinds of illicit drugs. And, you know, certainly now, the drugs that are out there are just scary. They're drugs that you can take once and end up dead. And that's really where the change has been. We recognize that there is an overlap between those systems, so we have a lot of stepdown care in DOD, a lot of intensive outpatient treatment, where we great both your mental health issues, which—PTSD runs with other things. It runs with TBI, it runs with depression, it runs with substance-use disorders, it runs with pain. And we also treat your substance-use disorders. With regard to opiate-use disorders, we've got medication-assisted therapy. With regard to alcohol-use disorders, lots of new science that supports the use of things like acamprosate, which is a medication-assisted therapy for alcoholism, or other drugs that work really well, like naltrexone.

Senator KING. So, you see this as an important area, that the co-morbidity is a significant issue.

Captain COLSTON. Oh, absolutely, sir. Dual-diagnosis work is really where most of our stepdown work is right now. And Walt, over at the NICoE, sees a fair amount of folks who are struggling in that regard, too.

Senator KING. Dr. Street, are there any VA rules that, if you— if you're suffering from PTSD, but you also have an—a drug-abuse problem, you can't get treatment, or you're excluded? There's no— there are no barriers on——

Dr. STREET. No, no barriers. And, in fact, increasingly, we're looking at treatments that can treat both of the disorders simultaneously, because we know that they are so interrelated.

Senator KING. A final question. I know that a program was created in 2010 to help people moving out of the service into—called In Transition, I think it's called. My question is, Is it working? And how do we know?

Captain COLSTON. So, we're collecting—that's run out of my office, sir—we're collecting data on it. We ramped up the program tenfold about a year ago.

Senator KING. Good.

Captain COLSTON. One of the things that we're trying to do throughout DOD is get outcome measures. And, luckily, there hasn't been, in this short period that we've been running the program, a suicide in any person who's been coached in the program. Nonetheless, we want outcome measures with regard to things like, How depressed is this patient? What kind of PTSD symptoms does this patient have? How much healthcare is this patient utilizing? And I think, as our health systems evolve, and as we develop registry data, the ability to get a better idea of where patients are as they move between DOD and VA, we'll get much better answers with regard to outcomes.

Senator KING. I think we should be applying the same level of resources, money and personnel, to transition out of the service that we put into recruiting in, because that's where a lot of the slippage occurs, in that sometimes very difficult transition. And that's been something I've—I just think that's a—that's a rule of thumb. Let's spend as much helping people when they come out as we spend bringing them in, in the first place.

Thank you very much for your testimony and for your work.

Senator GRAHAM. Senator Tillis.

Senator TILLIS. Thank you, Mr. Chair.

Thank you all for being here.

First off, I understand—I'm sorry I'm late. I had a competing— actually, I was just following Senator Sullivan through the committee, the concurrent committee circuit. So, I apologize for being late. If you've already answered these questions, I can just refer back to the record.

One thing I wanted to underscore, I think that Senator Sullivan covered. It's a bill that I support, the Fairness for Vets Act. I think you all got into a discussion here, so I won't ask you to repeat it, but just underscore, I think it—I think it's important, and I think it provides value. And I believe there's at least consensus among the Department that you do, as well? Thank you. Any problems with it?

Captain COLSTON. I haven't looked at it yet, sir.

Senator TILLIS. Okay. Okay.

And I think Senator Cotton may have mentioned something about public-private partnerships. We go to the easy—the easy one to identify, which would be the NFL [National Football League]. Based on where I come from, I could argue NASCAR [National Association for Stock Car Auto Racing]. But, what other sort of network of private partners are out there? And what, specifically, are we doing to really bring in and collaborate, use their expertise, not reinventing the wheel? And, Dr. Street, maybe I should direct that to you.

Dr. STREET. Yeah, there's actually a 2-day summit going on today and tomorrow that's really—the focus of it is public-private partnerships around the issue of TBI, and bringing in folks from VA, from DOD, the NFL, certainly researchers from the private sector who are familiar with those issues, to try to really garner innovative technologies from different sectors and apply them to this population.

I think that's a good general—this idea of public-private partnerships is a good general model, and one that VA is trying to do more and more of.

Senator TILLIS. Have we gone into any of the, maybe, research universities that do a lot of work there, and found partnership opportunities with them? Is that another area you're casting a net? Dr. STREET. Yeah, absolutely. I mean, where I hale from, in Boston, we have very close connections with Boston University. They've done a lot of work around chronic encephalopathy. And many of those investigators actually hold dual appointments in the academic institution and in VA so that we can really harness some of the power of the best scientists in the country who are doing this kind of work.

Senator TILLIS. Okay, thank you.

Senator King mentioned the transition piece. I'm on Veterans Affairs Committee. And, obviously, a lot of the challenges we have after a man or woman comes out, they may have undiagnosed TBI, PTSD. And I'm trying to figure out how we do a better job of—there's this handoff, and, you know, sometimes if you go in transition, you've got the younger soldiers that are in the back of the room with their headphones on, doing their duty, and then moving out there. They may be, in fact, people that should be listening. And what they're thinking about is moving on. To what extent is the DOD—it necessarily becomes a VA role, but to what extent is the DOD making sure that—particularly for ones where you may have evidence to suggest that someone does have something that has not yet been effectively treated—make sure that those veterans get vectored into the care that they may need through the VA? Does that handoff actually occur, or is it a—just because of the finite nature of the transition—I'm trying to get some sense of how we do a better job of making—the VA may not know that there is someone out there that may—they may need to help. So, it's—how do you kind of create an alert system—or does it already exist—to make sure there's a good handoff?

Captain COLSTON. Well, really, three things. First, there's a separation health assessment, where we try to cover all of these issues. For patients who present with any kind of condition, we have an Integrated Disability Evaluation System with the VA. And then we have an in-transition system to coach folks who—and it's an opt-out system, and it's not an opt-in system—to help folks get that next appointment.

I'd also say, for the sickest patients, we go all the way to—when I was at Great Lakes, if I had a 18-year-old patient with schizophrenia who was going to end up at the VA, one of my techs would get on the plane and bring him to Alabama or bring him to Texas. I mean, that's the level of transition support that's expected.

Senator TILLIS. Do you think that we're doing that consistently?

Captain COLSTON. Sir, I can say we're measuring it right now.

Senator TILLIS. Okay.

Captain COLSTON. And I could certainly take that question for the record as—with regard to how we're doing.

Senator TILLIS. Yeah, I would appreciate that. I mean, just to get some sense.

[The information referred to follows:]

In addition, August 2012, the Presidential Executive Order 13625 established the Interagency Task Force on Military and Veterans Mental Health (ITF) to implement mental health initiatives across the DOD, the Department of Health and Human Services, the VA, and other Federal agencies for Veterans, Service members, and their families. Specifically for Service members transitioning from the DOD to the VA system, one notable action has been the expansion of the DOD's *inTransition* program from "opt-in" participation, typically at the Separation Health Assessment, to "opt-out" or automatic enrollment. This program provides specialized coaching and assistance to all Service members seen for a mental health concern during the 12 months preceding their separation from military service. From inception in January 2010 and through March 2016, the *inTransition* program opened 16,484 new coaching cases and closed 13,821 coaching cases. Survey respondents continue to express high levels of satisfaction with *inTransition*, as 95 percent indicated the service met their needs, and 95 percent of the respondents indicated the assistance received from the program increased the likelihood of continuing treatment at the VA or with another clinical provider.

The DOD/VA Interagency Care Coordination Committee (IC3) addresses the needs of the most seriously wounded, ill, and injured Service members/Veterans and their families or caregivers. IC3, established in 2012, is improving the way DOD and VA care coordinators collaborate to provide more synchronized care, benefits, and services to those who require complex care coordination. IC3's synchronized efforts are supported by official policy in both Departments. Care coordination always includes point to point travel arrangements and by-name handoffs. This type of care is especially critical for the unfortunate Service members who develop serious life-long mental illnesses, such as schizophrenia or bipolar disorder. This high-needs population will require ongoing care regardless of the nation's war footing, as about 3 percent of the population develops these illnesses, with first presentations coinciding with typical age of military accession (18–25 years old).

Finally, an Integrated Disability Evaluation System has markedly increased the ability of DOD and VA to meet patients where they are, shortening wait times for disability determinations, and giving veterans options regarding where to access their follow-on care.

Senator TILLIS. You know, I'm from North Carolina. We've got a million veterans and a lot of folks who either serve at Fort Bragg or Lejeune that end up staying in North Carolina. And just want to make sure we're getting them to the care that we think can help avoid other problems and complications. I work a lot with a drug treatment facility down in Raleigh-Durham that's—about 60 percent of their clients are people who now have substance-abuse problems, but it's not clear how they got there, what caused them. Some of them are rooted in PTSD. So, I'm very sensitive to this issue to make sure we're capturing as many as possible and getting them in—into the appropriate sort of care setting. So, I would appreciate that.

Thank you, Mr. Chair.

Senator GRAHAM. Thank you.

This has been a excellent panel. I think you've all acquitted yourselves well.

Just to kind of summarize, one in four military members are affected by what we've been talking about today—trauma, PTS, drug abuse, alcohol-abuse problems. They've been treated for these problems. Is that correct?

Captain COLSTON. Yes, sir. We do a DMDC data run, so—a Defense Management Data Center data run—for everyone that's getting out, and look and say, "Have you been treated?"

Now, one thing I can say is, we're—we do a really good job with screening. And certainly, we've evolved to identify more of the illness that's out there. I think, you know, we now have probably the most treated cohort in human history. So——

Senator GRAHAM. Yeah, I would think so.

Captain COLSTON.—I think we're doing a good job in that regard.

Senator GRAHAM. Well, and that's the whole point. We want— you know, somebody asked this, but, you know, as I wrap up here and let other people ask additional questions, please tell us what we can do. Because, you know, we're trusting y'all guys. Everybody seems to be very focused that the veterans and those serving de- serve this.

About 80 percent of the cases are unrelated to being in combat.

TBI—one thing about the movie—I haven't seen it, but Senator Gillibrand was telling me—that you can't look at a TBI in-

jury on a MRI [Magnetic Resonance Imaging]. It's not like looking
at a broken bone, right?

Captain COLSTON. No, sir. There's no neural imaging, no correlation.

Senator GRAHAM. Only God knows how much of this we missed
in past conflicts.

Captain GREENHALGH. For the mild TBI, yes, sir.

Senator GRAHAM. Okay.

And I'll just add with this and let members wrap up what they
would like to ask.

I've been to a bunch of refugee camps. And I'd bet most of us
have. I can only imagine what the people in these refugee camps
are going through. From Syria—I was one in Turkey not long ago—
the children, the women, particularly, victims of sexual assault. So,
one thing, as a Nation, as a world, we need to—there's a—not a
whole lot of treatment, the people who have been through conflict.
And I just think they're ticking timebombs if we don't get ahead
of this. So, one thing I'd like the Senate to understand is that,
when we provide aid to the refugees, it's more than just food and
water and clothing. If we don't have a mental health component,
I think we're making a huge mistake.

So, anybody else?

Yes, Senator Sullivan.

Senator SULLIVAN. Just had a follow-up question.

So, the bill is actually S. 1567, Fairness to Veterans Erroneously
Discharged from the Military. That's the name of the bill. So, if you
could take a look at that to see if that's providing you additional
authorities that you think you need, which is obviously a issue that
seems to be a pretty big issue if you're looking at 200,000 cases. I
just had another question. Like Senator Tillis, I'm on the Veterans
Affairs Committee, and I asked the questions of some of our service
organizations when they were testifying recently. On the
designation PTSD, there's been some discussion of—you know, we
talk about the stigma, the "post-traumatic stress disorder." And so,
a "disorder" kind of comes with a little bit of, you know, implications. And so, some people have mentioned to me, "Well, maybe
we—this should be referred to as post-traumatic stress injury." So, if
you receive this in combat and you were injured, obviously, that it's
like, you know, getting shot. Nobody calls a gut wound or a— getting
shot a "disorder"; they call it a "injury." So—in some veterans
groups think that might be a good idea; others don't, for reasons
that might have to do with benefits and how things are actually
categorized in the VA. And if you don't call it a "disorder," you
might lose a certain amount of——

Do you have any thoughts on that, Dr. Street? Any of you? Just
on the—just the title, itself, which does have certain implications.
I was just wondering what your thoughts are on that.

Dr. STREET. I'm in favor of retaining the "post-traumatic stress
disorder" title. I appreciate the concern about stigma, but I—I don't
believe that changing the title is the way to most effectively combat
the stigma.

Senator SULLIVAN. No, I don't think it would at—I mean, I'm not
saying it would, but it—you know, it might be—might help, right?

Dr. STREET. I mean, I think certainly—just to outline my specific concerns—I mean, there is—we've made so much progress, in terms of our ability to diagnose and effective treat the disorder. And, in part, that's due to the fact that the symptoms of PTSD look so similar, regardless of the source of traumatic stress exposure, be that something associated with military service or something from the civilian sector. And I'm concerned that changing the name would introduce confusion that might negatively impact functioning. But, I agree that the issue of stigma is a concern and needs to be addressed. I'm just not sure that this is the most effective way to do it.

Captain COLSTON. There is a good point to the use of that term, inasmuch as the normal course of being exposed to trauma is toward health, and a vast majority of people who are exposed do get healthy. Sebastian Younger, in Vanity Fair, about a year ago, wrote a very beautiful article about some of his exposures and, you know, the subsequent course, and some of the things that we've seen in the military. It's tough to weather the vicissitudes of military life, especially when you're coming out of combat, especially when you're dealing with austere environments. But, I think that, you know, going back to where General Chiarelli was 5 years ago or so, when he used the term PTS as opposed to PTSD, there's arguments on both sides of the ledger.

I very much agree with Dr. Street's assertion that we've got to call it a "disorder," because we've got to get people services, we've got to get people support, and we've got to make diagnoses, to get paid, in the medical record.

Senator SULLIVAN. Thank you.

Senator GRAHAM. Yes, sir.

Senator TILLIS. This is really just to reinforce what the Chair said. One of the things that I'm really intent on is challenging you all to tell us where past congressional decisions at the time may have made sense; they may not have made sense, they just had the votes; or times have changed. But, the sorts of things that we place on you, particularly in dealing with this—you know, may end—well-intentioned policies that do not add value, they add cost or constraints. We need your feedback so that we're not only adding some new good ideas that maybe take the edge off of some of the old ones that are still in place, but really help us do reforms of any—you've got a very—you've got a changing environment. Your understanding of PTSD, how to treat it, how to transition, how to keep track of our vets and take care of them change over time. And I really want a committee where they come in here and you tell us, "You need to change this, this"—or call my office, or call the Chair's office, and give us an opportunity to look at some of the things that you're currently doing that are no longer value-added and could deploy resources to a better and higher use, in your professional opinion.

Senator GRAHAM. Thank you.

Anything else?

[No response.]

Senator GRAHAM. I move that all outside statements for the record received in advance of the hearing should be included in the official record. Without objection.

Senator GRAHAM. The hearing is adjourned. Well done. Thank you.

[Whereupon, at 3:47 p.m., the hearing was adjourned.]

[Questions for the record with answers supplied follow:]

1. Senator BLUMENTHAL. Captain Greenhalgh and Captain Colston: You state that the current policy of the Department of Defense (DOD) and Department of Veteran's Affairs (VA) is to conduct a "warm hand-off" for servicemembers' healthcare when they transition out of active duty service. What is the current status and effectiveness of the hand-off between the DOD and VA for servicemembers' healthcare, particularly concerning electronic records and pharmaceutical prescriptions?

Captain GREENHALGH and Captain COLSTON. Collaboration between DOD and the VA during the transition from DOD to VA health care has never been greater, and the two Departments are continuing their efforts to improve transition services. These services are mandated in policy and executed through intensive case management services, including an "InTransition" program to help Service members during the transition period.

Regarding electronic records, the Departments have collaborated on two complimentary mechanisms—a file transfer system and an electronic viewer—together they ensure all of the essential information of the DOD Health Record is available for both benefits adjudication and continuity of care in the VA. In 2010 the Departments agreed on the definition of the Service Treatment Records (STR)—it is the composite of all digital information and paper documentation necessary for continuity of care and benefits determinations. The STR includes the Armed Forces Health Longitudinal Technology Application (AHLTA), the Military Health System (MHS) electronic medical record that was implemented in 2004, and the older information that was created or is still printed on paper. To better enable claims processors in the VA to request and receive an official electronic archive version of the STR, DOD accelerated fielding of the DOD Health Artifact and Image Management Solution (HAIMS), and established an automated interface with systems supporting the Veterans Benefits Administration (VBA). Since January 1, 2014, the record transfer has occurred electronically. The Services compile and scan all the paper documentation and upload the files into HAIMS. In addition, everything from AHLTA is rendered as a single, well organized, easily searchable portable digital format (pdf) file. All of these files are stored in HAIMS and automatically copied from HAIMS to the VBA's system as soon as a claim is filed, completely eliminating the need to mail STR requests and printed copies of records between Departments. A July 2014, DOD Office of Inspector General report covered the period 6 months before and after the DOD HAIMS capability was put in place. The report compared the previous time preparing to mail a record with the current time to compile it into HAIMS, and did not highlight the time saved within the VA. Subsequent to this re- port, DOD and VA have significantly refined and improved on execution. The num- ber of VA late pending STR requests, which was over 6,000 in August 2014, has been consistently less than 1,000 since May 2015, and most STRs for new VA re- quests are now provided within one day of the date requested. The Services track late STRs by name until the request is closed out with the VA. DOD has imposed aggressive targets upon the Services, and they report compliance weekly.

The complimentary means of sharing the STR is through the electronic health information exchange that the Departments have been working on for a decade. Since December of 2013, everything from AHLTA has been accessible through the Joint Legacy Viewer (JLV), and constraints on system capacity were eliminated by the summer of 2015. JLV displays complete notes from AHLTA just as they appear when printed, a significant improvement over previous VA viewers. The viewer gives providers an integrated, chronological view of medical information familiar to clinicians of both Departments. It provides real-time electronic health record information from all DOD and VA facilities, as well as information received from a growing number of DOD and VA commercial health care partners. Today more than 70,000 VA clinicians have access to this system, a number that increased more than 60-fold in the past 15 months.

All of these improvements in health information access apply equally to Reserve Component Service members, and the archival process for them includes collecting and scanning any documentation held at the unit level.

Regarding pharmaceutical prescriptions, a just-released GAO audit, "Actions Needed to Help Ensure Appropriate Medication Continuation and Prescribing Practices," found no evidence to dispute a rigorous 2015 Veterans Health Administration study showing that 97 percent of transitioning Service members maintained clinically appropriate medication treatment through their transition from DOD to VA health care.

Beginning on June 1, in accordance with the National Defense Authorization Act for fiscal year 2016, section 715, "Joint Uniform Formulary for Transition Care," both the DOD and VA will be mandated to stock the same medications to treat pain, sleep, and psychiatric disorders, and any other conditions determined appropriate by the DOD and VA Secretaries. This synchronization will further ensure that patients leaving Active Duty have continuity of medication treatment during this transition.

Finally, DOD has worked closely with VA and HHS, and the Executive Office of the President, including the President's Office of National Drug Control Policy, to ensure that the President's mandates, vis-&-vis the potential for medication misuse, in Executive Order 13625 and subsequent 2014 Executive Actions are carried out. DOD is a national partner in the important effort to stem the scourge of prescription opiate abuse and overdose deaths. Integrated and extensive prescription drug monitoring programs, an extensive research portfolio coordinated between agencies, and execution of recent mandates in state and federal law will help turn the tide on this urgent public health problem.

VETERANS HEALTH ADMINISTRATION RESPONSE. The Department of Veterans Affairs (VA) has taken a number of actions in collaboration with the Department of Defense (DOD) to identify and track Servicemembers who are transitioning to civilian life and to ensure that those in need of care do not fall through the cracks. Enhanced health care information sharing has been accomplished through the DOD–VA Joint Legacy Viewer (JLV). JLV represents groundbreaking agency-to-agency interoperability. JLV combines and shares data and gives both VHA clinicians and Veterans Benefits Administration rating specialists a composite view of Veterans' treatment history.

VA's "Pilot Evaluation of Medication Continuation for Veterans Transitioning from the Department of Defense Health Care System to the Department of Veterans Affairs Health Care System" validated VA's long-standing practice of continuing medications for transitioning Servicemembers. This long-standing practice was institutionalized by VA with respect to mental health medications with the policy directive entitled, "Continuation of Mental Health Medications Initiated by Department of Defense Authorized Providers."

The link to the pilot evaluation is available at: *http://www.pbm.va.gov/PBM/vacenterformedicationsafety/othervasafetyprojects/DOD—VA—Medication—Continuation—Report.pdf*

The link to the VA Directive is available at: *http://www.va.gov/vhapublications/ViewPublication.asp?pub—ID=3075*

2. Senator BLUMENTHAL. Captain Greenhalgh, and Captain Colston: How do you plan to address the remaining shortfalls in the system?

Captain GREENHALGH and Captain COLSTON. Aside from issues regarding electronic health records and prescription drugs—including opiate overdose deaths nationwide, another concern that Department of Defense (DOD) and the Department of Veterans Affairs (VA) face is suicide deaths in recently discharged Service members.

The DOD's National Telehealth and Technology Center, a component of its Defense Centers of Excellence for Psychological Health and Traumatic Brain Injury (DCoE), expertly manages the DOD Suicide Event Report (DODSER), the most comprehensive database regarding death by suicide. Leaders at DCoE, in collaboration with VA researchers recently published a seminal article in the Journal of the American Medical Association regarding the relation of suicide risk to deployment and separation status. While deployment was not associated with the rate of suicide, separation from military service had a robust effect. The effect was pronounced in persons who separated with less than 4 years of military service or who did not separate with an honorable discharge.

In an effort to mitigate suicide risks by translating research findings into practice, then-Assistant Secretary of Defense for Readiness and Force Management promulgated the DCoE researchers' article to each of the Service's Assistant Secretaries for Manpower and Reserve Affairs (M&RA), with guidance to commanders to ensure a warm handoff to the Department of Labor for Service members who receive a less than honorable discharge. This handoff includes employment services and integration into social service systems, as appropriate, in the local community. The handoff is executed by name to ensure continuity between the commander, or his designee, and a Department of Labor representative at a specific American Job Center in the community. Additionally, *inTransition* is a free voluntary program to provide behavioral health care support to Service members and Veterans as they move between health care systems or providers. Personal coaches, along with resources and tools, assist participants during the transition period and empower them to make healthy life choices.

Recognizing risks associated with early separation while balancing readiness imperatives, the DOD has endeavored to drastically reduce separations of first-term Service members under the rubric of personality disorder, which does not carry the benefit of medical retirement. After policy was implemented in 2007, personality disorder separations were reduced from over 4,000 per year to 300 per year in 5 years. Each of the Service's Assistant Secretary for M&RA creates an annual report auditing the separation process for personality disorder; and the DOD has endeavored to listen to stakeholder's concerns about this matter over the past decade, including Veterans Service Organizations and representatives from the Yale Law Clinic. The change in policy carries a requirement to treat in place more Service members who are less able to weather the routine vicissitudes of military life. As such, the effort requires ongoing leadership and judgment from commanders, as the cohort of retained Service members presents risks for poor outcomes, including suicide. System-wide changes, such as the creation of service lines for mental health care and use of a behavioral health data portal, are designed to emphasize outcomes in the identification and management of those receiving mental health care.

It is important to note that a growing body of research suggests that mental health issues, such as depression or personality disorder, are only one part of a complex interplay of risk factors related to suicide. Suicide is a culmination of complex interactions between biological, social, economic, cultural and psychological factors operating at individual, community, and societal levels. Risk and protective factors span across the fields of medicine, epidemiology, sociology, psychology, criminology, education, and economics. Research also shows that many Service members and Veterans who are at risk for suicide will not seek help from mental health providers. Therefore, despite the efforts to improve access to clinical approaches, a suicide prevention response exclusively based on a mental health approach will not address suicide prevention efforts relevant to most of the at-risk population. A holistic, community approach that relies on a variety of interventions is more likely to increase effectiveness of suicide prevention efforts.

Defining suicide risk, and adequate treatment strategies, is an imperative in the DOD. Today, a $160 million military and operational medicine health research portfolio focuses on suicide. DOD integrates its suicide research efforts with other government agencies, especially VA and the Department of Health and Human Services (HHS), through the National Institute of Mental Health. A collaborative effort to improve understanding of suicide, along with Traumatic Brain Injury (TBI) and Posttraumatic Stress Disorder (PTSD), is focused in a National Research Action Plan (NRAP). The NRAP, mandated by an Executive Order in August 2012, created a roadmap to better coordinate and partition research portfolios to match agency expertise.

Comorbidity in military populations is becoming better understood, and research shows that TBI, PTSD, depression, substance use disorders, and chronic pain, are risk factors for suicide. The public health approach acknowledges the role of these various factors in suicide, but recognizes that these diagnoses can often be a result of other factors; for instance, pain and hopelessness that arise from other variables, such as relationship, financial, and legal problems; difficult transitions; and feelings of isolation. Therefore, addressing suicide with both clinical and non-clinical approaches provides the necessary multi-prong approach to address the various interconnected causal factors. Longitudinal research efforts like the Millennium Cohort Study, the largest study ever created to ascertain the health effects of military service, are slowly aiding scientific understanding to this issue.

There continues to be a comprehensive coverage of research portfolios across the DOD, VA, and HHS. Along with the epidemiological effort to collate and analyze annual suicide data in the annual DODSER, progress continues throughout the research continuum. While suicide prevention has been keenly focused upon by military leaders for many years, challenges still exist. One challenge is a low base rate for suicide, even in high risk groups making it difficult to target assistance to those who need it. Under the medical approach, the Army Study to Assess Risk and Resilience in Soldiers (Army STARRS) and its follow-on STARRS Longitudinal Study (efforts with projected outlays near $100 million), are attempting to enable clinicians to separate patients into risk cohorts, so interventions can be tailored according to risk. Additionally, randomized clinical trials under the auspices of a Military Suicide

Research Consortium are evaluating cognitive-behavioral suicide interventions in high risk groups, such as hospitalized patients. Another challenge is translating a vast body of research, containing a wealth of information about suicide prevention practices that have been tested and validated in different populations to the military. Using the public health approach, these practices are being reviewed, and some are piloted for implementation among Service members and Veterans. As an example, "Window to Hope" is an Australian program to reduce hopelessness that can lead to suicide after sustaining a traumatic brain injury. This program was recently adapted and evaluated for feasibility for U.S. military Veterans. Other studies have looked at components of post-traumatic stress disorder as a risk factor for suicide, finding that feelings of guilt and shame were underlying mechanisms of suicidal thoughts. Clinical trials now are underway to target these specific feelings.

The urgency of the suicide problem, with some military rates exceeding age-adjusted civilian rates for the first time in recent years, continues to push the DOD and VA's joint effort to develop effective prevention, intervention, and postvention strategies for suicide. It is necessary to maintain strong partnerships and collaborations during this process and ensure adequate communication. It is also crucial to use a public health approach in addition to addressing clinical factors related to suicide. The transition from active service is challenging and it is important to continue to forge the way in performing research, maintaining data, translating research findings into actionable outcomes and efforts, and measuring progress to address this vulnerable population and prevent suicides.

VETERANS HEALTH ADMINISTRATION RESPONSE. VA has multiple programs in place to facilitate transition from DOD and is continuously working to ensure that we monitor and respond to potential shortfalls in order to best meet the needs of our Veterans. For example, VA and DOD transition assets and capabilities supporting continuity between the health systems include liaison and care coordination staff to facilitate a seamless transition process, as well as numerous interagency initiatives that support shared standards of care and interoperable processes for care delivery that facilitate transition between the systems. For example, VA has 43 Liaisons for Healthcare stationed at 21 Military Treatment Facilities (MTF).

VA Liaisons for Healthcare, either licensed social workers or registered nurses, are strategically placed in MTFs with concentrations of recovering Servicemembers returning from Iraq and Afghanistan. VA Liaisons for Healthcare coordinate health care as Servicemembers transition from the MTF to a VA health care facility closest to their homes or the most appropriate location for the specialized services their medical condition requires. VA Liaisons are co-located with DOD case managers and provide onsite consultation and collaboration regarding VA resources and treatment options. VA Liaisons for Healthcare meet with Servicemembers directly to provide education about the VA system of care, the eligibility process, health care benefits, and services. They also assist in the understanding of the individual's health care needs in order to coordinate initial health care. VA Liaisons for Healthcare connect with Transition and Care Management Program Managers to coordinate this initial care and to have a VA case manager assigned.

VA Liaisons for Healthcare facilitate the connection between the DOD and VA case managers and treatment teams, ensuring that current health care needs are communicated. The expectation with each referral is that the Servicemember will leave the MTF registered for VA health care with a scheduled VA appointment. Since this connection has been made prior to leaving the MTF, the Servicemember is already engaged with Transition and Care Management Program Managers upon arrival home. This early connection with Servicemembers and their families/caregivers starts the process of building a positive relationship with VA and ensures early coordination of health care with VA.

VA has also coordinated with DOD's *inTransition* program to receive Servicemembers separating from the service who have been seen by a mental health provider while on Active Duty or who self-refer to the inTransition program. This DOD program provides coaching to assist Servicemembers who are transitioning between health care systems, status, or locations. inTransition's mission is to support continuity of care for the Servicemember during transition. A transition coach provides support and guidance on psychological health concerns, resources, and healthy living, while motivating and assisting the Servicemember to connect with a treatment provider post-transition. In the second quarter of fiscal year 2016, *inTransition* opened 1,900 new coaching cases. From February 2010 to March 2016, the cumulative number of coaching cases opened by the *inTransition* program was 16,509. Survey respondents expressed high levels of satisfaction with *inTransition*, with 89 percent indicating the assistance received from the program increased their likelihood of continuing treatment at the new location and 90 percent indicating that *inTransition* products and services met their needs.

The link to the *inTransition* program is available at: http://intransition.dcoe.mil/

Statement for the Record

Daniel R. Weinberger, M.D.
Director and Chief Executive Officer
Lieber Institute for Brain Development/Maltz Research Laboratories

On

Current State of Research, Diagnosis, and Treatment for Post-traumatic Stress
Disorder and Traumatic Brain Injury

Before the
Committee on Armed Services
Subcommittee on Personnel
United States Senate

April 20, 2016

Thank you Subcommittee Chairman Graham and Ranking Member Gillibrand for holding this important hearing and for the opportunity to submit testimony on the current state of research, diagnosis, and treatment for post-traumatic stress disorder (PTSD) and traumatic brain injury (TBI).

I am a Professor in the Departments of Psychiatry, Neurology, Neuroscience and the McKusick-Nathans Institute of Genetic Medicine at the Johns Hopkins School of Medicine, as well as the Director and Chief Executive Officer of the Lieber Institute for Brain Development/Maltz Research Laboratories (LIBD), an independent, not-for-profit medical research institution founded in 2010 in affiliation with Johns Hopkins School of Medicine. LIBD's mission is to translate the understanding of basic genetic and molecular mechanisms of brain disorders into therapeutic interventions that will change the lives of affected individuals and their families. Our study of the genetic and epigenetic mechanisms of brain disorders, such as schizophrenia, has led us to new understandings of the entire spectrum of neuropsychiatric disorders, including the mechanisms of brain dysfunction in TBI, the identification of biomarkers for PTSD, and more importantly, the development of innovative and potentially life-saving treatments for those suffering from these debilitating conditions. To accomplish this, we are leveraging the world's largest repository of donated post-mortem human brains, coupled with extensive genetic and molecular analysis, medical histories and demographic information about the donors, and broadly sharing our findings with researchers across the globe through our open-access *BrainCloud*.

There are currently limited pharmacological treatments for PTSD and TBI. New treatment options are urgently needed, especially medications that target the cognitive and behavioral symptoms of individuals suffering from PTSD and TBI such as memory loss, depression, diminished executive function, impulsivity, addiction, increased risk of violence and, most tragically, suicide. At LIBD, we are seeking ways to accelerate the development of treatments for PTSD, TBI, and comorbidities by identifying the mechanisms unique to these disorders at the cellular and molecular levels.

PTSD and TBI Disproportionately Affect Servicemen and Veterans

As the Subcommittee is aware, PTSD and TBI have a disproportionate effect on our active duty servicemen and veterans. It has been six years since the RAND Corporation's Center for Military Health Policy Research published its ground-breaking study revealing the extensive prevalence of PTSD among previously deployed Operation Enduring Freedom and Operation Iraqi Freedom (Afghanistan and Iraq) service members.[1] RAND concluded that 18.5 percent of all returning service members met the criteria for either PTSD or depression. The men and women who have served our country in combat suffer from PTSD at alarmingly higher rates than the 7.3 percent rate estimated for the general population.[2]

In addition, our foreign combat operations have resulted in high rates of TBI and blast-related concussions, which directly impact the long-term health and well-being of our combat forces, their families, and our communities. RAND concluded that 19.5 percent of service members surveyed reported experiencing a probable TBI during deployment.[3] TBI can cause injuries resulting in lifelong consequences, including increased risk of suicide, substance abuse, mood disorders, changes in personality, loss of self-regulation of behavior, increases in violent behavior and domestic violence, and impaired thinking and memory.

1 Tanielian, T. & Jaycox, L. (Eds.) "Invisible Wounds of War: Psychological and Cognitive Injuries, Their Consequences, and Services to Assist Recovery." RAND Corporation, Santa Monica, CA (2008) (RAND Invisible Wounds Report); see also Institute of Medicine. Treatment for Posttraumatic Stress Disorder in Military and Veteran Populations: Final Assessment. Washington, DC: The National Academies Press, 2014. doi:10.17226/18724.

2 A. L. Roberts, S. E. Gilman, J. Breslau, N. Breslau and K. C. Koenen, "Race/Ethnic differences in exposure to traumatic events, development of post-traumatic stress disorder, and treatment-seeking for post-traumatic stress disorder in the United States," *Psychological Medicine* (Vol. 41 Issue 1) January 2011, pp 71-83.

3 RAND Invisible Wounds Report (2008).

The cost to our society is enormous. RAND estimated in 2008 that PTSD-related and major depression-related costs could range from $4.0 to $6.2 billion over two years.[4] The costs incurred for TBI within the first year after diagnosis were estimated between $591 million and $910 million. RAND included costs only for diagnosed TBI cases that led to contact with the health care system; not the costs for individuals with probable TBI who have not sought treatment or who have not been formally diagnosed, or the costs associated with chronic or recurring cases lasting more than two years, let alone the costs resulting from lost productivity and lives lost to suicide, or the costs to families, employers and communities resulting from the co-morbidities associated with depression and substance abuse.[5] Estimates for the present value of the cost of care over 40 years range from $57 billion to $717 billion.[6]

Sadly, recent studies show that the risk of suicide attempts is particularly high among people with TBI and PTSD. Twenty-seven percent of people diagnosed with PTSD will attempt suicide.[7] Those who defend our country are at the highest risk of PTSD/TBI-related suicide. With 22 veteran suicides a day, America is losing far more veterans to suicide than to recent combat operations.

To date, the majority of public discussion and scientific research has focused on how the brain is damaged by TBI and PTSD, why individuals living with these disorders respond poorly to therapeutic interventions over the course of time, and how we can prevent brain injuries. While diagnosis and prevention efforts are crucial, it is imperative that we accelerate the search for effective treatments for individuals after the acute stages after injury, to improve cognition, restore behavioral control, stabilize mood and reduce the impulsivity that can lead to acts of violence, rage and addictions. The principal challenges confronting us are not only to understand how a brain gets damaged, but more fundamentally, to discover ways to improve the function of the brain parts that have escaped damage. The availability of post-mortem brains, from both impacted and non-impacted donors, along with skilled research and real-time sharing of discoveries, is essential to meeting this challenge.

The Urgent Need for Translational Research on PTSD and TBI

Given the disproportionate impact of TBI and PTSD on our society, and particularly on our active duty service members and veterans, it is essential that we devote the resources necessary to better understanding the structural and molecular changes in the damaged brain. A better

4 Statement of Lisa H. Jaycox, Ph.D., Senior Behavioral Scientist/Clinical Psychologist and Study Co-Director, Invisible Wounds of War Study Team, RAND Corporation, "Invisible Wounds of War: Summary of Key Findings on Psychological and Cognitive Injuries," Testimony before the House Committee on Veterans' Affairs, June 11, 2008 (RAND Testimony), available at...

5 Rand Testimony.

6 L. Kille, "Cost of long-term medical benefits to Afghanistan and Iraq veterans," January 4, 2013, available at...

7 Sareen, J., Cox, B.J., Stein, M.B., Afifi, T.O., Fleet, C., & Asmundson, G.J.G. (2007). Physical and mental comorbidity, disability, and suicidal behavior associated with posttraumatic stress disorder in a large community sample, Psychosomatic Medicine, 69, 242-248. doi: 10.1097/PSY.0b013e3180316bd8

understanding of these changes, and the identification of potential biomarkers for determining susceptibility at the cellular and molecular levels, can lead to innovative and effective treatments that will help them rebuild their lives and maybe their brains.

The greater the availability of donated post-mortem brains, coupled with genetic and molecular analyses, extensive medical histories, demographic information about the donors and broadly-shared scientific data, the higher the probability that we will identify new targets for effective treatments – and even potential cures – as rapidly as possible while our service members and veterans are still living. LIBD has dedicated significant resources to developing the largest and most carefully curated and characterized collection of human brains for the study of development and neuropsychiatric disorders in history. Our team is collecting an average of five brains every week. The repository consists of over 2,100 brains of individuals with various neuropsychiatric disorders, as well as control cases crucial to basic research. For each consented case we acquire, we collect extensive medical histories, environmental and demographic information, toxicological analyses, individual personality and psychiatric histories, and family information. In addition to this unprecedented tissue resource, the same team of individuals who have worked together with standardized procedures for over 15 years, process and diagnose all samples. Further, the same person dissects all brains for research. This builds in an unprecedented degree of standardization, which is fundamental to minimizing the influence of confounders and noise factors in the data.

Since the inception of the LIBD brain repository, we have also accumulated the largest collection of confirmed cases of PTSD brains for research in the world, as well as hundreds of brains of individuals who have committed suicide. We are proud to serve as the exclusive brain tissue resource for the Department of Veterans Affairs' Leahy-Friedman National PTSD Brain Bank, which launched in 2015. Access to extensively characterized brain tissue has enabled researchers across the USA to identify potential genes and biomarkers that can answer why some individuals are more susceptible to PTSD after a traumatic experience, while others are not. We have already discovered how one genetic variant thought to increase risk for PTSD, influences the function of the brain. More insights about the biology of the susceptible brain is likely to follow, and as funding becomes available we will work to translate these molecular clues into novel treatments.

LIBD is also fulfilling a critical research gap in developing novel treatments for TBI. To date, the vast majority of research funding has been on the prevention, detection, and acute phase treatment of repeated concussions and TBI. LIBD is developing a novel treatment for the long-term effects of TBI, which are the most disabling and costly to the individual, their families and society at large. Of the more than 6,000 cases of TBI a day, more than 60 percent of the affected individuals will have long-term disabilities related to their head trauma. Currently available treatments are woefully inadequate. New approaches to mitigate these effects are urgently needed.

Translating Research to Cures

Our "bench to bedside" approach is designed to translate basic scientific findings into therapeutic interventions for individuals suffering from brain disorders. We have broken through the traditional silos between basic and clinical research. The impact of our work, and the strategic acquisition of the brain tissue needed for research, is underscored by our growing partnerships with federal agencies such as the National Institutes of Health, Department of Defense, Department of Veterans' Affairs, and leading academic institutions such as the Johns Hopkins University, Columbia University, Case Western Reserve University, Stanford, Harvard, Duke, the University of Colorado, and the University of Miami. We have also established major collaborations with international medical research centers, including at Peking University and Seoul National University.

We have also established a pre-competitive consortium with seven leading pharmaceutical manufacturers specializing in developing neuropsychiatric treatments to speed the process of translating research about the brain into novel treatments for brain disorders. Our quest to understand the biological roots of behavioral problems has already led to an innovative therapeutic trial for a drug aimed at TBI that targets how the brain self-regulates behavior, and particularly how various regions of the brain control impulsiveness and aggressiveness. While still early, we are hopeful our efforts will encourage other researchers to seek new and innovative approaches to solving what has been until recently an insoluble problem for individuals with TBI and related disorders.

Brain Cloud - A Public Scientific Resource

Beginning as a collaboration with the National Institute of Mental Health, LIBD is making genetic, biological, and clinical data available to researchers around the world at no cost. *BrainCloud* is an internet application that allows scientists to explore the temporal dynamics and genetic control of transcription in the human brain across the lifespan (the process by which genes are turned on and off during normal and abnormal brain development). Our goal for *BrainCloud* is to generate a better understanding of the genetic variations that confers risk for brain disorders, and susceptibility to PTSD following traumatic events, which will spur the discovery of new treatments. The broad availability of data through *BrainCloud* is a major step forward in implementing the ambitious goals set by this Congress and the Administration as part of precision medicine initiatives and the Brain Research through Advancing Innovative Neurotechnologies (Brain Initiative).

Potential for Future Research

Investment in drug discovery and in a target development pipeline will accelerate efforts to find novel treatments for traumatic brain injury and other neuropsychiatric disorders. LIBD's most advanced program is the development of inhibitors of catechol-O-methyltransferase (COMT), an important enzyme for metabolizing dopamine in the cortex of the brain. COMT plays a critical role in regulating memory and self-control of behavior and is a highly attractive target for improving brain function in individuals with TBI. While useful for pilot studies, the only currently available COMT inhibitor that gets into the brain is tolcapone, which has major clinical issues, including risk of liver toxicity that prevents widespread use. Tolcapone also has a very short half-life and requires administration three to four times per day.

Other COMT inhibitors that do not get into the brain are widely used in the treatment of Parkinson's disease to reduce peripheral metabolism of l-dopa, the principal anti-Parkinson's therapy. Experience with these compounds has completely de-risked the target of COMT inhibition, which is safe and without adverse effects. The data with tolcapone, though critically limited, has shown consistent central nervous system effects to improve cognition, emotional regulation and behavioral control. The LIBD has a mature drug discovery program where our medicinal chemists have prepared novel inhibitors of COMT such as LI-48X that are currently progressing through efficacy and safety testing that will support human clinical trials. These compounds have long half-lives permitting once daily dosing and are highly brain penetrant. Dependent on available funding, one of the new COMT inhibitors could be in clinical testing in less than two years.

Conclusion

When our servicemen and veterans fall victim to TBI and PTSD, they deserve all the tools the best science can provide so they can recover and live full lives when they return home. We urge the Committee to focus on the areas of greatest scientific promise and need, including the type of innovative and translational research LIBD is conducting to help for those struggling with these debilitating disorders. A strengthened investment of funding for basic and translational research into the molecular biology of PTSD and TBI, as well as strategic acquisition of post-mortem brains for research, will close the gap between basic research and clinical implementation to prevent and counter the effects of PTSD and TBI. We are on the threshold of discoveries that will change the lives of the brave American men and women who have served, and continue to serve, our great country. We can do no less for those coping now with invisible wounds from service to our country, and pave the way for those who will serve in the future.

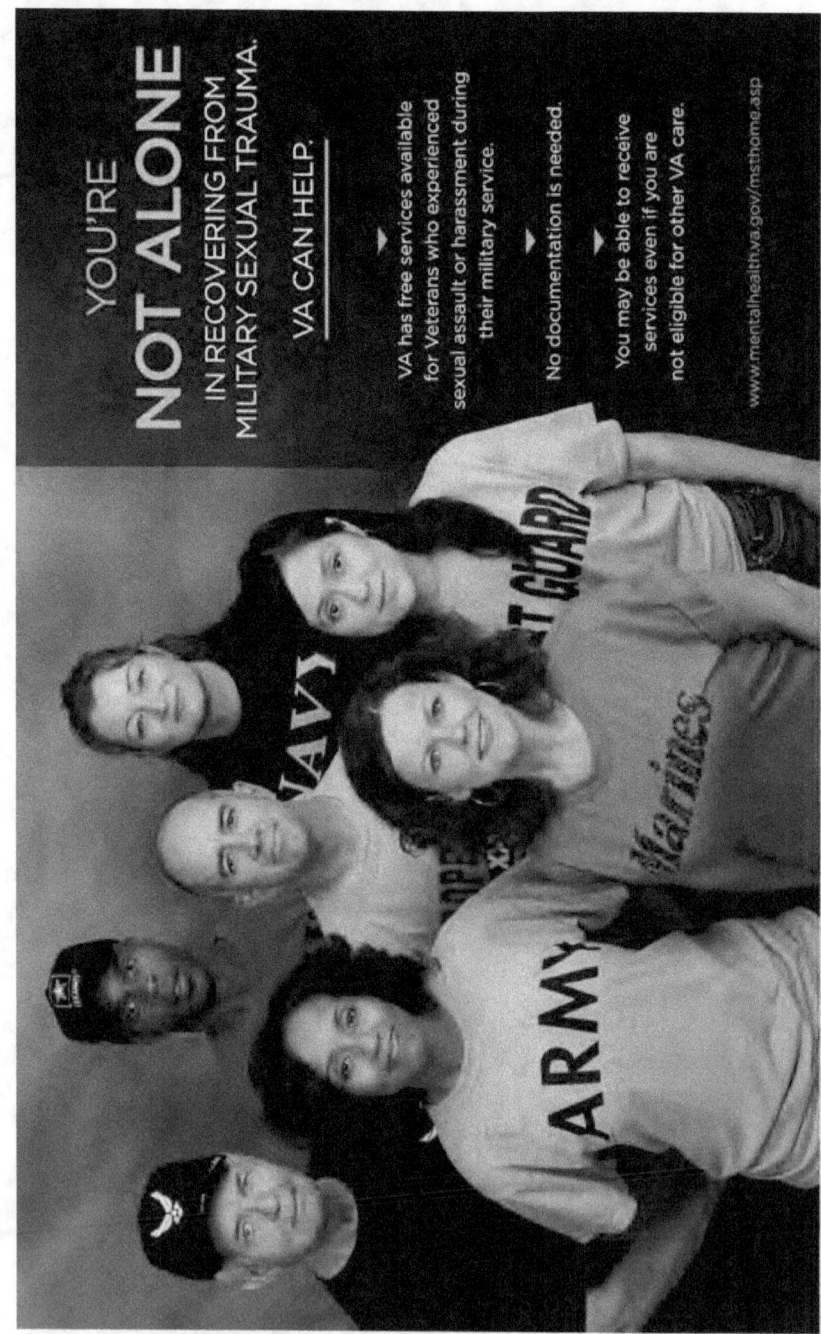

YOU'RE NOT ALONE

IN RECOVERING FROM MILITARY SEXUAL TRAUMA.

VA CAN HELP.

▸ VA has free services available for Veterans who experienced sexual assault or harassment during their military service.

▸ No documentation is needed.

▸ You may be able to receive services even if you are not eligible for other VA care.

www.mentalhealth.va.gov/msthome.asp

FOR MORE INFORMATION,
CONTACT YOUR FACILITY'S MST COORDINATOR

Trauma sexual militar

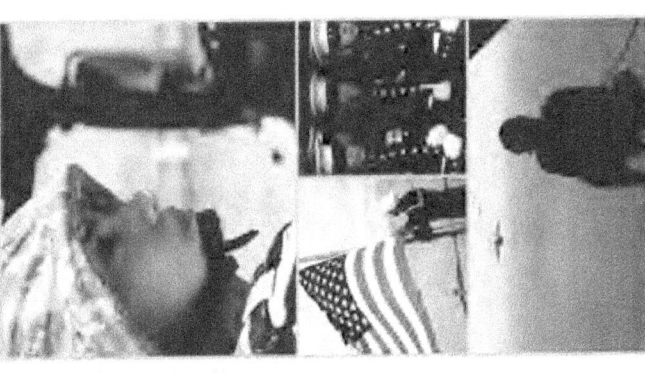

Para mas información pueden hablar con su proveedor de cuidado de salud, o contactar al coordinador de servicio a personas que han sufrido trauma sexual durante su servicio militar (Coordinador de MST), o a cualquier centro local de servicios al veterano (Centro de Veteranos).

Para localizar el centro de servicios al veterano más cercano, favor de llamar al **1-800-827-1000** o vía internet a través de **www.va.gov** o **www.vetcenter.va.gov** donde encontrará un listado de los centros de servicios al veterano

Usted puede solicitar hablar con un profesional de su mismo sexo o sexo opuesto si esto le hace sentir más cómodo.

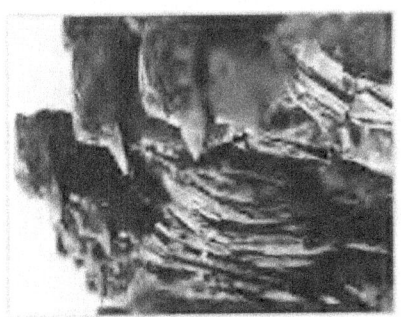

Tanto hombres como mujeres pueden estar expuestos a algún tipo de trauma sexual durante su servicio militar. Cualquier tipo de trauma puede afectar la salud física y mental del individuo. Por tal razón, todos los veteranos atendidos en cualquiera de las facilidades de salud de la Administración de Veteranos se les pregunta si durante los años de servicio militar ellos tuvieron expuestos a algún tipo de trauma sexual. Es de conocimiento que una persona se pueda recuperar de cualquier trauma. Por eso la Administración de Salud al Veterano tiene servicios disponibles para ayudar a personas a recuperarse.

VETERANO:

¿Has estado expuesto a alguna situación donde ha recibido una atención o avance sexual no deseado, o sexo forzado durante su servicio en las fuerzas armadas?

¿Sigue esta experiencia afectando su vida en la actualidad?

mst

U.S. Department of Veterans Affairs

Veterans Health Administration

Septiembre 2010

44

¿QUÉ ES EL TRAUMA SEXUAL MILITAR?

El Trauma Sexual Militar conocido como MST por sus siglas en inglés es el término usado por el Departamento de Asuntos del Veterano para referirse a agresión o acoso sexual ocurrido mientras un veterano estuvo en las fuerzas armadas. Esto incluye cualquier actividad sexual donde una persona es participe en contra de su voluntad. El o ella ha podido ser obligado(a) a participar en una actividad sexual por medio de amenazas con consecuencias negativas. Por ejemplo, no recibir una promoción o mejor tratamiento si rehúsa tener relaciones sexuales. También ha podido estar no capacitada(o) a consentir a ningún tipo de actividad sexual si por ejemplo la persona está intoxicada o ha sido físicamente obligada(o) a tener sexo. Otras experiencias bajo la categoría de trauma sexual militar incluyen el tocar o agarrar sexualmente a alguien en contra de su voluntad; hacer comentarios amenazantes u ofensivos acerca del cuerpo o actividades sexuales de una persona; y/o avances sexuales amenazantes e indeseados.

El MST puede afectar la salud física y mental de una persona a través de los años. Algunas de las dificultades que tanto hombres como mujeres sobrevivientes de MST pueden tener son:

* **Emociones fuertes:** Sentirse deprimido; reacciones emocionales repentinas a cosas; sentirse enojado(a) o irritado(a) todo el tiempo

* **Sentimientos de inseguridad:** Indiferencia emocional; dificultad para sentir y expresar emociones como el amor o la felicidad

* **Dificultad al dormir:** Dificultad para dormir y mantenerse dormido; pesadillas

* **Dificultad en mantenerse atento y concentrado;** dificultad con la memoria

* **Problemas con alcohol u otras drogas**

* **Dificultades con cosas que les recuerden la experiencia de trauma sexual;** Nerviosidad; tensión; inseguridad; evitar recordar la experiencia traumática y dificultad en confiar en los demás

* **Dificultad en relaciones con otras personas;** Sentirse aislado y desconectado de otras personas; relaciones abusivas; problemas con empleadores y figuras de autoridad

* **Problemas de salud física;** Dificultades sexuales; dolor crónico; problemas de peso o alimenticios; problemas gastrointestinal

¿QUÉ SERVICIOS HAY DISPONIBLES?

La Administración de Veteranos provee servicios confidenciales de consejería y tratamiento completamente gratis a hombres y mujeres veteranos que sufren de problemas físicos y mentales relacionados a sus experiencias de trauma sexual mientras servían en las fuerzas armadas. Aunque no sea elegible para recibir cuidado médico a través de la Administración de Veteranos, puede recibir este beneficio de consejería y tratamiento. No es necesario el que haya reportado el incidente cuando ocurrió, o que haya documentado lo ocurrido para recibir éste servicio.

¿PUEDO SOLICITAR BENEFICIOS DE COMPENSACIÓN POR DISCAPACIDAD, POR CONDICIONES RELACIONADAS A MI EXPERIENCIA DE TRAUMA SEXUAL MIENTRAS SERVÍA EN LAS FUERZAS ARMADAS?

Como veterano usted puede recibir compensación por discapacidades que comenzaron o empeoraron mientras servía en las fuerzas armadas. Esto incluye discapacidades y lesiones como resultado de trauma sexual militar. Cuando un veterano solicita servicio de compensación por discapacidad, la Administración de Veteranos debe determinar, primeramente si la discapacidad actual está relacionada con su servicio militar. De ser así, la compensación se basará en el nivel de impedimento presente.

Un representante de la Administración de Beneficios al Veterano (VBA) puede explicarle y proveerle información detallada sobre el programa de compensación, y ayudarle a llenar y someter papeles para un reclamo. Para más información, llame a la línea directa de la Administración de Veteranos al **1-800-827-1000.**

Military Sexual Trauma

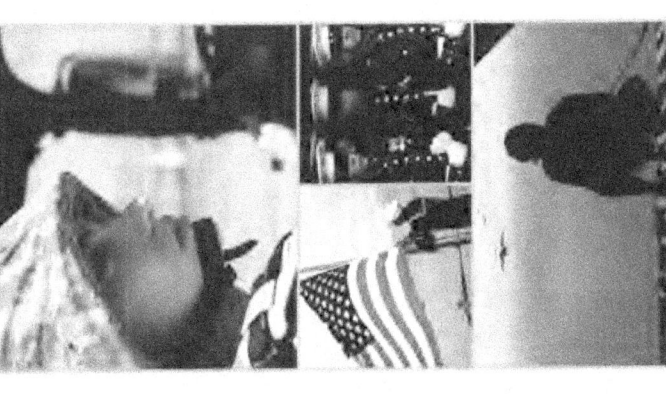

For more information, male and female veterans can speak with their existing VA healthcare provider, contact the MST Coordinator at their nearest VA Medical Center, or contact their local Vet Center.

A list of VA and Vet Center facilities can be found online at

www.va.gov and

www.vetcenter.va.gov.

You can also call VA's general information hotline at 1-800-827-1000 or visit www.mentalhealth.va.gov/msthome.asp

Veterans should feel free to ask to meet with a clinician of the same or opposite sex if it would make them feel more comfortable.

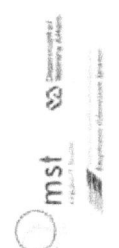

VETERANS:

Did you experience any unwanted sexual attention, uninvited sexual advances, or forced sex while in the military?

Does this experience continue to affect your life today?

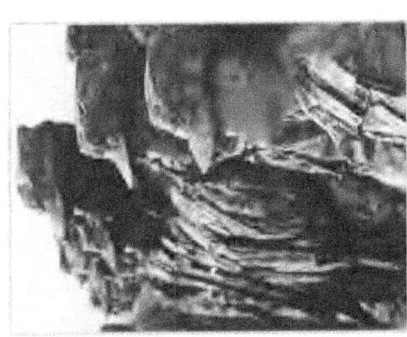

Both women and men can experience military sexual trauma (MST) during their service. All veterans seen at Veterans Health Administration facilities are asked about experiences of sexual trauma because we know that any type of trauma can affect a person's physical and mental health, even many years later. We also know that people can recover from trauma. VA has services to help veterans do this.

WHAT IS MILITARY SEXUAL TRAUMA?

Military sexual trauma (MST) is the term that the Department of Veterans Affairs uses to refer to sexual assault or sexual harassment that occurred while the veteran was in the military. It includes any sexual activity where someone is involved against his or her will - he or she may have been pressured into sexual activities (for example, with threats of negative consequences for refusing to be sexually cooperative or with implied faster promotions or better treatment in exchange for sex), may have been unable to consent to sexual activities (for example, when intoxicated), or may have been physically forced into sexual activities. Other experiences that fall into the category of MST include unwanted sexual touching or grabbing; threatening, offensive remarks about a person's body or sexual activities; and/or threatening and unwelcome sexual advances.

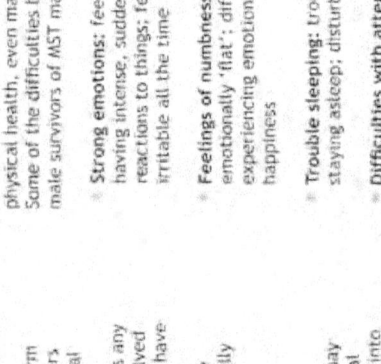

MST can affect a person's mental and physical health, even many years later. Some of the difficulties both female and male survivors of MST may have include:

* **Strong emotions:** feeling depressed; having intense, sudden emotional reactions to things; feeling angry or irritable all the time

* **Feelings of numbness:** feeling emotionally 'flat'; difficulty experiencing emotions like love or happiness

* **Trouble sleeping:** trouble falling or staying asleep; disturbing nightmares

* **Difficulties with attention, concentration, and memory:** trouble staying focused; frequently finding their mind wandering; having a hard time remembering things

* **Problems with alcohol or other drugs**

* **Difficulty with things that remind them of their experiences of sexual trauma:** feeling on edge or 'jumpy' all the time; difficulty feeling safe; going out of their way to avoid reminders of their experiences; difficulty trusting others

* **Difficulties in relationships:** feeling isolated or disconnected from others; abusive relationships; trouble with employers or authority figures

* **Physical health problems:** sexual difficulties; chronic pain; weight or eating problems; gastrointestinal problems

WHAT SERVICES ARE AVAILABLE?

The VA provides free, confidential counseling and treatment to male and female veterans for mental and physical health conditions related to experiences of MST. You do not need to be service connected and may be able to receive this benefit even if you are not eligible for other VA care. You do not need to have reported the incident when it happened or have other documentation that it occurred.

CAN I APPLY FOR DISABILITY COMPENSATION FOR CONDITIONS RELATED TO MY EXPERIENCES OF MST?

Veterans can receive compensation for disabilities that began or got worse in the line of duty, including disabilities or injuries resulting from MST. When a veteran applies for disability compensation, VA must first determine whether there are current disabilities related to his or her military service. If there are compensation is based on the current level of impairment.

A Veterans Service Representative at the Veterans Benefits Administration (VBA) can explain the compensation program in greater detail and assist you in filing a claim. For more information, call the VA's general information hotline at **1-800-827-1000.**

TOP 10 THINGS ALL HEALTHCARE &
SERVICE PROFESSIONALS SHOULD KNOW ABOUT

VA SERVICES for SURVIVORS of
MILITARY SEXUAL TRAUMA

1. **Military sexual trauma (MST) is a term used by the Department of Veterans Affairs to refer to sexual assault or repeated, threatening sexual harassment that occurred during a Veteran's military service.** MST can occur on or off base and while a Veteran is on or off duty. Perpetrators can be men or women, military personnel or civilians, commanding officers or subordinates, strangers, friends, or intimate partners. Veterans from all eras of service – from World War II to those who served more recently in Iraq and Afghanistan – have reported experiencing MST.

2. A significant number of men and women report having experienced MST. About one in five women and one in 100 men have told their VA healthcare provider that they experienced sexual trauma in the military. Though rates of MST are higher among women, because of the high ratio of men to women in the military there are in fact only slightly less men than women seen in VA that have experienced MST.

3. **MST affects both mental and physical health.** Sexual assault is more likely to result in symptoms of PTSD than are most other types of trauma, including combat. Symptoms of depression and substance abuse are also common. Sexual trauma can also have severe consequences for physical health and is associated with higher rates of headaches, gastrointestinal difficulties, sexual dysfunction, chronic pain, and chronic fatigue. Even survivors who do not experience problems at the level of formal diagnosis may still struggle in certain situations with emotional reactions, memories related to their experiences of MST, or interpersonal issues. Recovery is possible, however, and VA has services to help Veterans with this.

4. VA has responded to MST in a variety of ways. Since 1992, the VA has been developing initiatives to improve our ability to identify MST survivors and ensure that they have access to specialized care. For example, all Veterans seen in VA healthcare settings are asked if they experienced MST. All treatment for physical and mental health conditions related to MST is free. VA engages in outreach to Veterans about services available and ensures that staff receive training on MST-related issues. As with disabilities related to other experiences during military service, Veterans can receive compensation for disabilities or injuries resulting from MST.

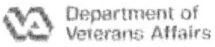
Department of
Veterans Affairs

mst

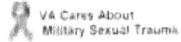
VA Cares About
Military Sexual Trauma

5. **In VA, treatment for all mental and physical health conditions related to MST is free and unlimited in duration.** Veterans do not need to have a disability rating (that is, be 'service-connected'), to have reported the incident(s) at the time, or to have other documentation that MST occurred in order to receive free MST-related care. There are no time limits on eligibility for this care, meaning that Veterans can seek out treatment even many years after discharge.

6. **Veterans may be eligible for free MST-related care even if they are not eligible for other VA services.** There are special eligibility rules associated with MST-related care and many of the standard requirements related to length of service or financial means do not apply.

7. **VA has specialized treatment programming available for MST survivors.** VA facilities have providers knowledgeable about evidence-based mental health care for the aftereffects of MST. Many have specialized outpatient mental health services focusing on sexual trauma. Vet Centers also have specially trained sexual trauma counselors. For Veterans who need more intensive treatment and support, there are programs nationwide that offer specialized sexual trauma treatment in residential and inpatient settings.

8. **VA knows that MST survivors may have special treatment needs and concerns.** For example, a Veteran can ask to meet with a clinician of a particular gender if it would make him or her feel more comfortable. Similarly, to accommodate Veterans who do not feel comfortable in mixed-gender treatment settings, many facilities throughout VA have separate programs for men and women. All residential and inpatient programs have separate sleeping areas for men and women.

9. **Every VA facility has an MST Coordinator who serves as a point person for MST-related issues.** He or she can tell you about treatment and other resources available in your area. Contact your local VA facility for more information.

10. **There are several ways Veterans can get help.** For more information, Veterans can speak with their existing VA healthcare provider, contact the MST Coordinator at their nearest VA Medical Center, or contact their local Vet Center. A list of VA and Vet Center facilities can be found online at www.va.gov and www.vetcenter.va.gov. Veterans and others can also call VA's general information hotline at 1-800-827-1000. More information about MST is available at http://www.mentalhealth.va.gov/msthome.asp.

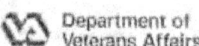 Department of Veterans Affairs mst 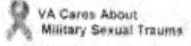 VA Cares About Military Sexual Trauma

July, 2010

VA Cares About Military Sexual Trauma

You can contact this facility's
MST Coordinator

_____

at

_____

VA HEALTH CARE | EXCELLENCE

VA Cares About Military Sexual Trauma

You can contact this facility's
MST Coordinator

_____

at

_____

VA HEALTH CARE | EXCELLENCE

VA Cares About Military Sexual Trauma

You can contact this facility's
MST Coordinator

_____

at

_____

VA HEALTH CARE | EXCELLENCE

VA Cares About Military Sexual Trauma

You can contact this facility's
MST Coordinator

_____

at

_____

VA HEALTH CARE | EXCELLENCE

VA Cares About Military Sexual Trauma

You can contact this facility's
MST Coordinator

_____

at

_____

VA HEALTH CARE | EXCELLENCE

VA Cares About Military Sexual Trauma

You can contact this facility's
MST Coordinator

_____

at

_____

VA HEALTH CARE | EXCELLENCE

VA Cares About Military Sexual Trauma

You can contact this facility's
MST Coordinator

_____

at

_____

VA HEALTH CARE | EXCELLENCE

VA Cares About Military Sexual Trauma

You can contact this facility's
MST Coordinator

_____

at

_____

VA HEALTH CARE | EXCELLENCE

VA Cares About Military Sexual Trauma

You can contact this facility's
MST Coordinator

_____

at

_____

VA HEALTH CARE | EXCELLENCE

VA Cares About Military Sexual Trauma

You can contact this facility's
MST Coordinator

_____

at

_____

VA HEALTH CARE | EXCELLENCE

PEOPLE CAN RECOVER FROM TRAUMA.
To help Veterans do this, VA provides
free, confidential treatment
for mental and physical health conditions related
to experiences of sexual assault or sexual harassment
during military service. You do not need
to have a VA disability rating and
may be able to receive this treatment
even if you are not eligible for other VA care.

For more information, visit www.mentalhealth.va.gov/msthome.asp

PEOPLE CAN RECOVER FROM TRAUMA.
To help Veterans do this, VA provides
free, confidential treatment
for mental and physical health conditions related
to experiences of sexual assault or sexual harassment
during military service. You do not need
to have a VA disability rating and
may be able to receive this treatment
even if you are not eligible for other VA care.

For more information, visit www.mentalhealth.va.gov/msthome.asp

PEOPLE CAN RECOVER FROM TRAUMA.
To help Veterans do this, VA provides
free, confidential treatment
for mental and physical health conditions related
to experiences of sexual assault or sexual harassment
during military service. You do not need
to have a VA disability rating and
may be able to receive this treatment
even if you are not eligible for other VA care.

For more information, visit www.mentalhealth.va.gov/msthome.asp

PEOPLE CAN RECOVER FROM TRAUMA.
To help Veterans do this, VA provides
free, confidential treatment
for mental and physical health conditions related
to experiences of sexual assault or sexual harassment
during military service. You do not need
to have a VA disability rating and
may be able to receive this treatment
even if you are not eligible for other VA care.

For more information, visit www.mentalhealth.va.gov/msthome.asp

PEOPLE CAN RECOVER FROM TRAUMA.
To help Veterans do this, VA provides
free, confidential treatment
for mental and physical health conditions related
to experiences of sexual assault or sexual harassment
during military service. You do not need
to have a VA disability rating and
may be able to receive this treatment
even if you are not eligible for other VA care.

For more information, visit www.mentalhealth.va.gov/msthome.asp

PEOPLE CAN RECOVER FROM TRAUMA.
To help Veterans do this, VA provides
free, confidential treatment
for mental and physical health conditions related
to experiences of sexual assault or sexual harassment
during military service. You do not need
to have a VA disability rating and
may be able to receive this treatment
even if you are not eligible for other VA care.

For more information, visit www.mentalhealth.va.gov/msthome.asp

PEOPLE CAN RECOVER FROM TRAUMA.
To help Veterans do this, VA provides
free, confidential treatment
for mental and physical health conditions related
to experiences of sexual assault or sexual harassment
during military service. You do not need
to have a VA disability rating and
may be able to receive this treatment
even if you are not eligible for other VA care.

For more information, visit www.mentalhealth.va.gov/msthome.asp

PEOPLE CAN RECOVER FROM TRAUMA.
To help Veterans do this, VA provides
free, confidential treatment
for mental and physical health conditions related
to experiences of sexual assault or sexual harassment
during military service. You do not need
to have a VA disability rating and
may be able to receive this treatment
even if you are not eligible for other VA care.

For more information, visit www.mentalhealth.va.gov/msthome.asp

PEOPLE CAN RECOVER FROM TRAUMA.
To help Veterans do this, VA provides
free, confidential treatment
for mental and physical health conditions related
to experiences of sexual assault or sexual harassment
during military service. You do not need
to have a VA disability rating and
may be able to receive this treatment
even if you are not eligible for other VA care.

For more information, visit www.mentalhealth.va.gov/msthome.asp

PEOPLE CAN RECOVER FROM TRAUMA.
To help Veterans do this, VA provides
free, confidential treatment
for mental and physical health conditions related
to experiences of sexual assault or sexual harassment
during military service. You do not need
to have a VA disability rating and
may be able to receive this treatment
even if you are not eligible for other VA care.

For more information, visit www.mentalhealth.va.gov/msthome.asp

 **You are not alone in overcoming military sexual trauma**

Veterans of all backgrounds have experienced MST, regardless of factors such as physical size, age, race, or sexual orientation.

Military sexual trauma (MST) is sexual assault or sexual harassment that occurred during a Veteran's military service:

- Being pressured into sexual activities, such as with threats
- Sexual activities without your consent, such as when asleep or intoxicated
- Being overpowered or physically forced to have sex
- Being sexually touched or grabbed in a way that made you uncomfortable, including during hazing experiences
- Repeated comments about your body or sexual activities
- Threatening and unwelcome sexual advances

COMMON STRUGGLES REPORTED BY MEN

 MASCULINITY WORRIES

 SEXUAL CONCERNS

 RELATIONSHIP PROBLEMS

 ANGER

 SHAME

RECKLESS BEHAVIOR

 SLEEP TROUBLE

 CHRONIC PAIN

 PANIC OR ANXIETY

MST IS NEVER YOUR FAULT

YOU ARE NOT ALONE

Almost half of all Veterans who tell a provider they experienced MST are men.

It takes a lot of **COURAGE** and **STRENGTH** to speak up.

There are many steps you can take to  **MOVE FORWARD** after MST.

IT'S NEVER TOO LATE, AND IT'S NEVER TOO SOON

- VA has free MST-related services available for Veterans
- You may be able to receive MST-related services even if you are not eligible for other VA care

- No documentation of the MST experience is needed to get care
- Every VA has an MST Coordinator to help access services and resources
- Contact your local facility and ask to speak to the MST Coordinator for more information

Visit **www.mentalhealth.va.gov/msthome.asp** to learn more about MST and the recovery programs and services available at VA.

 mst

 VA

Written Testimony of Edmond Richer, Associate Professor, Southern Methodist University

Hearing of the United States Senate Armed Services Committee, Subcommittee on Personnel: Current State of Research, Diagnosis, and Treatment for Post-Traumatic Stress Disorder and Traumatic Brain Injury

April 20, 2016

Ground Breaking Research in Brain Trauma Prediction and Prevention at SMU

Brain Blast Injury (BBI) is the leading cause of traumatic brain injury (TBI) in military personnel. TBI has considerable economic, military and social implications. Blast injuries are frequently caused by the high overpressure blast waves generated by improvised explosive devices (IEDs). Neurologists estimate that at least 30% of military personnel who have engaged in active combat for more than four months are at risk of potentially disabling neurological disorders despite not sustaining external injury. These soldiers will live for many decades with the neurological series of sequelae ranging from PTSD to traumatic encephalopathy

Most researchers have focused on linear and angular accelerations of the head and their effect on brain tissue deformation, without being able to reliably predict the risk of injury and delayed neurological disorders. It has been documented that brain injuries occur not only in areas adjacent to the skull, as explained by the coup-countercoup injury mechanism, but also at relatively large depths within the brain tissue. This suggests more subtle injury mechanisms, not based on direct contact and viscoelastic deformation of the brain tissue under external accelerations.

Recent research carried out at SMU shows that head collisions in contact sports generate elastic waves that produce high strain and stress concentrations in the brain tissue, despite the use of protective helmets. Similarly, blast waves propagating through the head can create complex pressure gradients and overpressure concentrations in the intracranial volume, which can induce tissue stresses and strains that can cause localized damage to deep brain tissue. This hypothesis is supported by the few available animal experiments, which have shown that exposure to even low blast overpressure levels impairs the performance of rats in cognitive tests. Evidence of small hemorrhages in the brain tissue and signs of brain edema were seen in pigs which had been exposed to blasts.

SMU is working on realistic multi-physics finite element analysis (MPFEA) 3D models of the brain, skull and helmet based on medical imaging techniques that can be rapidly analyzed using SMU's supercomputer, SMU-HPC. This research will lead to better understanding of the mechanisms of blast wave injuries to deep brain tissue.

Our research team at SMU developed ultrasensitive micro-photonic Whispering Gallery Mode (µWGM) sensors that can be embedded in brain tissue phantoms without perturbing the measurements. This will allow for the first time the experimental validation of the overpressure concentrations inside the brain, predicted by theoretical analysis.

Moreover, the elastomer additive manufacturing system (elastomer 3D printing) developed at SMU has the ability to accurately reproduce anatomical features with realistic mechanical properties based on medical images of military personnel. This unique set of expertise and research equipment allows a novel and highly effective approach for understanding and solving this important problem.

The success of this project will provide better understanding of blast injuries and facilitate new protective equipment designs. This will lead to better protection and rapid recovery of soldiers from the effect of blasts in the battlefield. Additionally, it will facilitate better diagnostics, medical care, and rehabilitation of soldiers with TBI and enable significant economic benefits from reduced medical costs and more productive lives.

Further information is included in the attached paper, *Analysis of sports related mTBI injuries caused by elastic wave propagation through brain tissue*, Dave Case and Edmond Richer, The International Journal of Multiphysics, Volume 9, Number 1 (2015).

Contact:

Volkan Otugen
Senior Associate Dean
Lyle School of Engineering
Southern Methodist University
otugen@lyle.smu.edu
(214) 768-3255

Analysis of sports related mTBI injuries caused by
elastic wave propagation through brain tissue

by

David Case and Edmond Richer

reprinted from

THE INTERNATIONAL JOURNAL OF
MULTIPHYSICS

2015: VOLUME 9 NUMBER 1

MULTI-SCIENCE PUBLISHING

Int. Jnl. of Multiphysics Volume 9 · Number 1 · 2015

Analysis of sports related mTBI injuries caused by elastic wave propagation through brain tissue

David Case and Edmond Richer*
Biomedical Instrumentation and Robotics Laboratory,
Southern Methodist University

ABSTRACT
Repetitive concussions and sub-concussions suffered by athletes have been linked to a series of sequelae ranging from traumatic encephalopathy to dementia pugilistica. A detailed finite element model of the human head was developed based on standard libraries of medical imaging. The model includes realistic material properties for the brain tissue, bone, soft tissue, and CSF, as well as the structure and properties of a protective helmet. Various impact scenarios were studied, with a focus on the strains/stresses and pressure gradients and concentrations created in the brain tissue due to propagation of waves produced by the impact through the complex internal structure of the human head. This approach has the potential to expand our understanding of the mechanism of brain injury, and to better assess the risk of delayed neurological disorders for tens of thousands of young athletes throughout the world.

1. INTRODUCTION

In recent years, mild traumatic brain injury (mTBI) has received more and more attention due to the large number of high school, college, and professional athletes affected during sporting events. Repetitive concussions and sub-concussions have been linked to a series of sequelae ranging from traumatic encephalopathy to dementia pugilistica [1–3].

It has been documented that brain injuries occur not only in areas adjacent to the skull, as predicted by the coup/counter-coup models, but also at relatively great depths within the brain tissue. This suggests a more subtle injury mechanism, not based on direct contact deformation under external stresses.

Numerous researchers focused on linear and angular accelerations of the head and the associated effects on brain tissue deformation (see [1, 3–5] and references therein). They used reconstruction of impacts from game videos or accelerometer-based telemetry systems as input data, derived brain tissue stress/strain distribution from sophisticated finite element (FE) computer models, and validated their models on mannequins or cadavers in order to assess the risk of injury [3, 4, 6, 7]. These studies suggest that transient gradients of the stresses/strains within the brain tissue are the root cause of later neurological dysfunctions.

While a lot of attention has been given to the brain injury due to direct contact phenomena and to the effect of linear and angular accelerations of the head during an impact, very few studies have examined the effect of wave propagation through the brain tissue [8–10]. Moreover, none of these studies were conducted in the context of sports-specific injuries.

*Corresponding Author: E-mail: richer@smu.edu

Int. Jnl. of Multiphysics Volume 9 · Number 1 · 2015

Analysis of sports related mTBI injuries caused by elastic wave propagation through brain tissue

David Case and Edmond Richer*
Biomedical Instrumentation and Robotics Laboratory,
Southern Methodist University

ABSTRACT
Repetitive concussions and sub-concussions suffered by athletes have been linked to a series of sequelae ranging from traumatic encephalopathy to dementia pugilistica. A detailed finite element model of the human head was developed based on standard libraries of medical imaging. The model includes realistic material properties for the brain tissue, bone, soft tissue, and CSF, as well as the structure and properties of a protective helmet. Various impact scenarios were studied, with a focus on the strains/stresses and pressure gradients and concentrations created in the brain tissue due to propagation of waves produced by the impact through the complex internal structure of the human head. This approach has the potential to expand our understanding of the mechanism of brain injury, and to better assess the risk of delayed neurological disorders for tens of thousands of young athletes throughout the world.

1. INTRODUCTION

In recent years, mild traumatic brain injury (mTBI) has received more and more attention due to the large number of high school, college, and professional athletes affected during sporting events. Repetitive concussions and sub-concussions have been linked to a series of sequelae ranging from traumatic encephalopathy to dementia pugilistica [1–3].

It has been documented that brain injuries occur not only in areas adjacent to the skull, as predicted by the coup/counter-coup models, but also at relatively great depths within the brain tissue. This suggests a more subtle injury mechanism, not based on direct contact deformation under external stresses.

Numerous researchers focused on linear and angular accelerations of the head and the associated effects on brain tissue deformation (see [1, 3–5] and references therein). They used reconstruction of impacts from game videos or accelerometer-based telemetry systems as input data, derived brain tissue stress/strain distribution from sophisticated finite element (FE) computer models, and validated their models on mannequins or cadavers in order to assess the risk of injury [3, 4, 6, 7]. These studies suggest that transient gradients of the stresses/strains within the brain tissue are the root cause of later neurological dysfunctions.

While a lot of attention has been given to the brain injury due to direct contact phenomena and to the effect of linear and angular accelerations of the head during an impact, very few studies have examined the effect of wave propagation through the brain tissue [8–10]. Moreover, none of these studies were conducted in the context of sports-specific injuries.

*Corresponding Author: E-mail: richer@smu.edu

57

2. FINITE ELEMENT MODELING

2.1 MODELING BASED ON MR IMAGES AND SEGMENTATION

Our work is aimed to improve the existing FE models used to predict the effect of impact on the brain, by taking into consideration the strains/stresses and pressure gradients created in the brain tissue by the propagation of elastic waves produced by the impact. Due to the complex internal structure of the human head, containing tissues with intricate anatomy and vastly different mechanical properties (from bone to cerebral spinal fluid (CSF)), multiple reflections, refractions, interferences, and resonant phenomena are expected. These in turn have the potential to create sharp moving pressure and strain gradients as well as areas of stress concentration that will increase the risk of brain tissue damage and the probability of future neurological sequelae.

To test the feasibility of the proposed approach we built a detailed model of the helmet/head system based on standard medical Magnetic Resonance (MR) brain images. Without loss of generality, a two-dimensional model was assembled, based on the CT scan of a human adult from the front of the head, focused at the midbrain (Fig. 1a). Image segmentation was used to differentiate between brain structures, skull, various types of soft tissue, and the CSF. The primary bony structures seen in this cross-section are the parietal and temporal plates of the skull and the mandible. Between the bony protrusions of the mandible are the soft tissues of the throat, tongue, and pallet. Finally, the brain itself is shown, with apparent lateral and third ventricles, surrounded by cerebral fluid. Encasing the skull is a thin layer of soft tissue, representing the skin (Fig. 1b). The FE model was augmented with a protective helmet represented by a configuration of foam rubber pads and impact plastic in direct contact with the skin. The entire assembly was surrounded by an air environment. As shown in Table 1, the model includes realistic material properties of the brain as well as the other head tissues: bone, soft tissue, skin, and CSF [3, 11]. The protective helmet padding was modeled as foam rubber and the shell as impact plastic.

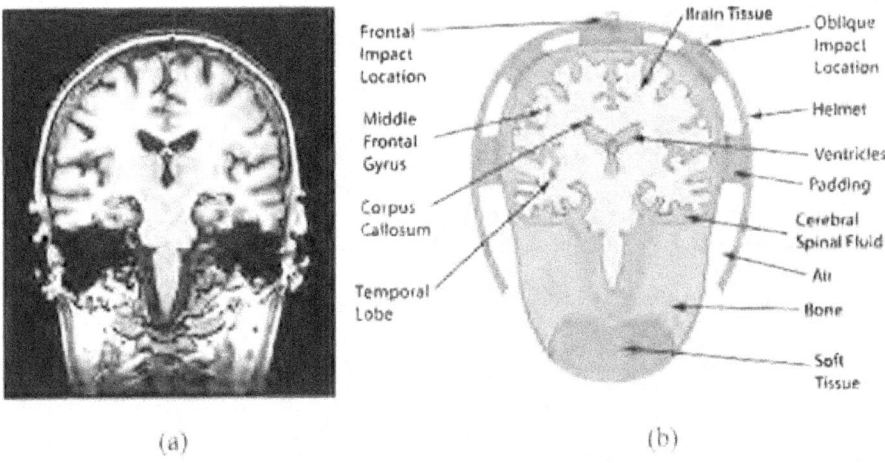

(a)   (b)

Figure 1: Modeling based on anatomical MR images of a human head focused on the midbrain (a) and tissue identification based on image segmentation (b). Points of particular interest for measurement are indicated in red (from top to bottom: middle frontal gyrus, corpus callosum, and temporal lobe at the lateral sulcus)

Int. Jnl. of Multiphysics **Volume 9 · Number 1 · 2015**

Table 1: Material properties for biological tissues and protective helmet

Material	Density ρ [kg/m³]	Speed of Sound c [m/s]
Air	1.1225	340
Bone	2,100	3,200
CSF	1,040	1,433
Soft Tisssue	1,000	1,540
Foam Rubber	1,190	60
Impact Plastic	1,190	2,870

2.2 SIMULATION PHYSICS

The Acoustic-Solid Interaction Module of COMSOL Multiphysics (COMSOL Inc., Burlington, MA) was used for time-dependent FE analysis. The solid domains were modeled as linear elastic material, subject to

$$\rho \frac{\partial^2 u}{\partial t^2} - \nabla \cdot \sigma = Fv \tag{1}$$

where u is a displacement vector, Fv represents any external strains or loads, and the scalar σ term is the double dot product of the strain tensor and a Rayleigh damping matrix, derived as follows:

$$\sigma = C_p : (\varepsilon) = \Sigma_i \Sigma_j C_{inj} \varepsilon_{jj} \tag{2}$$

$$C_p = \alpha_{dM} m + \beta_{dk} k + C \tag{3}$$

where m and k are the mass and stiffness matrices of the material, respectively, and $\alpha_{dM} = 1/80$ s^{-1} and $\beta_{dk} = 0.0003$ s are the associated damping parameters. The remaining "weak static" contribution, C, is the elasticity tensor derived from the associated material's Young's modulus and Poisson's ratio.

For the fluid domain a time-varying pressure field was modeled based on the following wave equation:

$$\frac{1}{\rho c^2} \frac{\partial^2 p}{\partial t^2} + \nabla \cdot \left(-\frac{1}{\rho}(\nabla p - q) \right) = Q \tag{4}$$

Here, ρ and c represent the density and speed of sound within the local material, p represents the local pressure, and q and Q represent any present dipole or monopole source terms, respectively.

The boundary condition defined between the solid and fluid domains is as follows:

$$\sigma \cdot n = pn \tag{5}$$

$$-n \cdot \left(-\frac{1}{\rho}(\nabla p - q) \right) = -n \cdot u \tag{6}$$

where n is the outward pointing unit normal vector, as seen from inside the solid domain. These equations define the fluid loads on the solid domain and the structural acceleration's effect on the fluid.

In the assembled model, a monopole source term is placed at the outer surface of the helmet, above the second foam pad on the right-hand side for oblique impact analysis and directly above the third pad for frontal impact analysis. These represent two possible impact scenarios during the sporting activity. The source is given a Gaussian time profile.

$$Q = -A\, 2\pi^2 f^2 (t - t_p)\, e^{-\pi^2 f^2 (t - t_p)^2} \qquad t_p - 1/f < t < t_p + 1/f \qquad (7)$$

with amplitude $A = 1$ m²/s, frequency bandwidth $f = 100$Hz, f and pulse peak time $t_p = 0.01$s. The outer limits of the surrounding air domain are given a "plane wave –radiation" boundary condition to allow outgoing waves to leave the modeling domain without reflection:

$$-\mathbf{n} \cdot \left(-\frac{1}{\rho}(\nabla p - \mathbf{q}) \right) + \frac{1}{\rho}\left(\frac{1}{c}\frac{\partial p}{\partial t} \right) = Q \qquad (8)$$

2.3 MESHING

The FE mesh for oblique impact analysis is shown in Fig. 2 and consisted of 56,794 triangular elements, with size adjusted automatically according to the complexity of the anatomical features. The mesh for frontal impact analysis was comparable, consisting of 56,896 triangular elements. The relevant statistics and parameters for both models are as follows: Minimum Element Quality – 0.3552; Average Element Quality – 0.9323; Maximum Growth Rate – 2.755 (oblique)/3.064 (frontal); Average Growth Rate – 1.406.

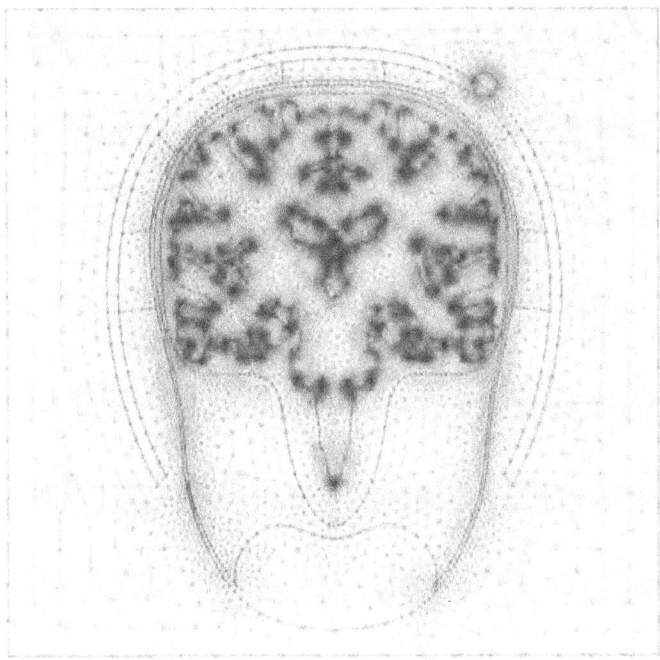

Figure 2: Finite element mesh consisting of 56,794 triangular elements

Int. Jnl. of Multiphysics **Volume 9 · Number 1 · 2015**   5

3. SIMULATION RESULTS AND ANALYSIS

A Dell OptiPlex 7010 work station with 3rd Gen Intel Quad Core i5-3470, and 16 GB DDR3, 1600 MHz RAM was used to run the time-dependent *Multifrontal Massively Parallel sparse direct Solver* (MUMPS). The time interval was set for 100 ms after impact, with 0.1 ms steps, and a scaled absolute tolerance of 0.001. A *Fully Coupled* node that uses a damped version of Newton's method was employed with *Termination technique* set to a *Tolerance factor* = 1.

The results of the time-dependent analysis for the oblique impact scenario are shown in Fig. 3. Post-processing reveals the propagation of the acoustic wave (with sound level in dB) through the helmet and head. The results for the air domain are not shown to increase the clarity of the results in the areas of interest. As expected, the initial wave rapidly progresses through the helmet and head. Due to the small wave attenuation through the CSF and brain tissue [11], the wave is reflected and refracted multiple times at the interfaces between the inner surface of the skull, auditory system, and internal brain structures. Sharp gradients and pressure foci develop in the temporal lobes, frontal Gyri, and corpus callosum starting 15 ms after impact and lasting for approximately 50 ms (see Fig. 3c – 3h). In some of these areas the absolute pressure can even exceed the maximum value at the impact site, as seen in Fig. 4. Furthermore, these maximum values are dependent upon the location of the impact site. A peak impact presssure value of 1,000 Pa at an oblique angle on the surface of the helmet produces a 2,700 Pa peak value in the temporal lobe with an oblique impact scenario and a 3,500 Pa peak value with a frontal impact scenario (Fig. 5).

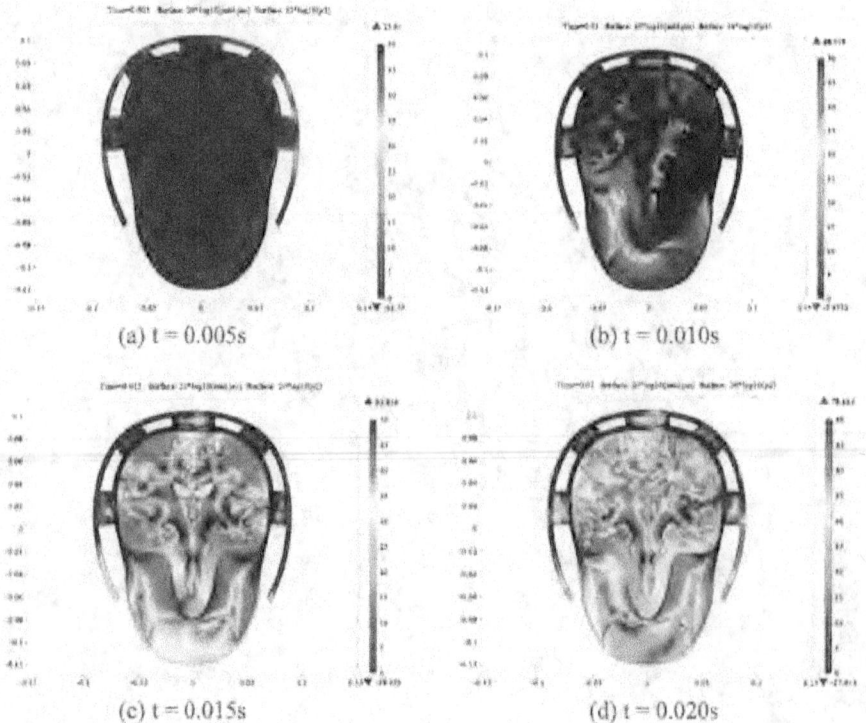

(a) t = 0.005s

(b) t = 0.010s

(c) t = 0.015s

(d) t = 0.020s

Figure 3: (Continued)

61

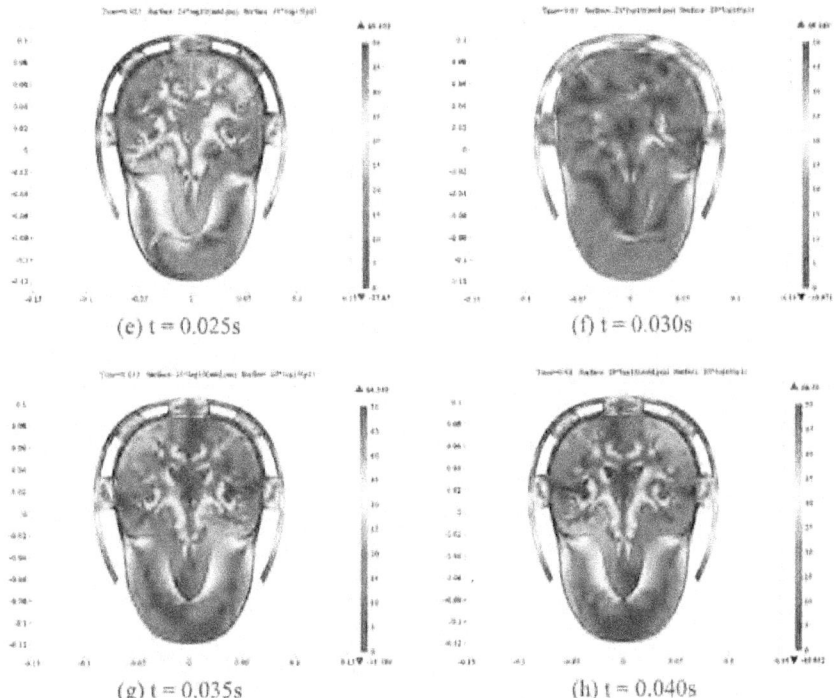

(e) t = 0.025s   (f) t = 0.030s

(g) t = 0.035s   (h) t = 0.040s

Figure 3: Time series (*t* = 0 – 40) of finite element simulation results showing the sound level in decibels

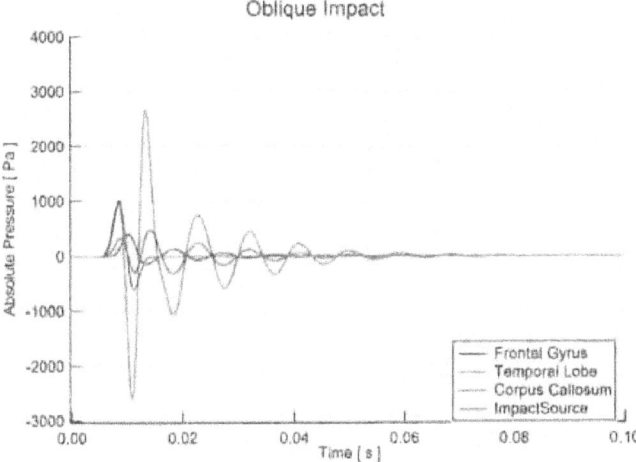

Figure 4: Absolute pressure foci in selected areas of the brain in reaction to an oblique impact

Int. Jnl. of Multiphysics **Volume 9 · Number 1 · 2015**

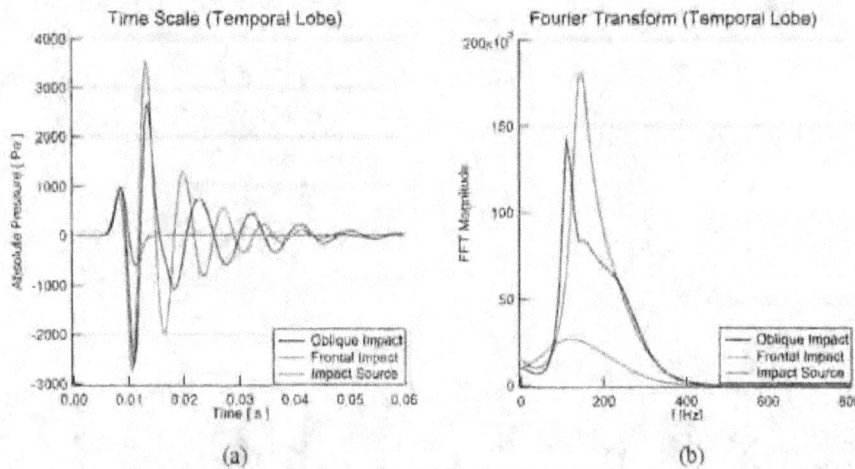

Figure 5: Comparison of pressure focus in the temporal lobe under oblique and frontal impact scenarios. Pressure focus is shown on a time scale (a) and with frequency composition (b)

4. CONCLUSIONS

We developed a detailed FE model of an athlete's head based on standard libraries of medical imaging. The model includes realistic material properties of the brain tissue, bone, soft tissue, and CSF, as well as a protective helmet. The results show that foci of intense pressure concentration are formed in specific areas of the brain, possibly exceeding the maximum pressure applied to the helmet surface. These pressure foci are dependent upon the location of impact and have the potential of inducing significant strains and stresses that would supplement the ones predicted by acceleration-based analysis.

The detailed time domain FE analysis of the pressure wave propagation through the athlete's head has the potential to expand our understanding of the mechanism of brain injury and improve the accuracy of mTBI prediction. Moreover, it opens the ability to create personalized models of mTBI based on MR images of individual players and real time game impact data. This can lead to better assessment of risk of injury and of delayed neurological disorders for tens of thousands of young athletes throughout the world.

REFERENCES

[1] Dashnaw, M., Petraglia, A. and Bailes, J., 2012. "An overview of the basic science of concussion and subconcussion: where we are and where we are going". Neurosurgical Focus, 33, pp. 1–9.

[2] Kelly, J., Amerson, E. and Barth, J., 2012. "Mild traumatic brain injury: Lessons learned from clinical, sports, and combat concussions". Rehabilitation Research and Practice, 2012, pp. 1–5.

[3] Viano, D., Casson, I., Pellman, E., Zhang, L., King, A. and Yang, K., 2005. "Concussion in professional football: Brain responses by finite element analysis: Part 9". Neurosurgery, 57, pp. 891–915.

[4] Funk, J., Rowson, S., Daniel, R. and Duma, S., 2012. "Validation of concussion risk curves for collegiate football players derived from HITS data". Annals of Biomedical Engineering, 40, pp. 79–89.

[5] Meaney, D. and Smith, D., 2011. "Biomechanics of concussion". Clinical Sports Medicine, 30, pp. 19–31.

[6] Willinger, R., Kang, H.-S. and Diaw, B., 1999. "Three-dimensional human head finite-element model validation against two experimental impacts". Annals of Biomedical Engineering, 27, pp. 403–410.

[7] Schatz, P. and Zillmer, E., 2003. "Computer-based assessment of sports-related concussion". Applied Neurophsychology, 10, pp. 42–47.

[8] Clayton, E., Genin, G. and Bayly, P., 2010. "Wave propagation in the human brain and skull imaged in vivo by MR elastography". In Proceedings of the International Federation for Medical and Biological Engineering.

[9] Yin, X. and Hynynen, K., 2005. "A numerical study of transcranial focused ultrasound beam propagation at low frequency". Physics in Medicine and Biology, 50, pp. 1821–1836.

[10] Shahsavari, S., McKlevey, T., Ritzen, C. and Rydenhag, B., 2011. "Cerebrovascular mechanical properties and slow waves of intracranial pressure in TBI patients". IEEE Transactions on Biomedical Engineering, 58, pp. 2072–2082.

[11] Kremkau, F., Barnes, R. and McGraw, C., 1981. "Ultrasonic attenuation and propagation speed in normal human brain". The Journal of the Acoustical Society of America, 70, pp. 29–38.

A CELL-FREE NANOTHERAPEUTIC BRAIN GLUE FOR TRAUMATIC BRAIN INJURY REPAIR

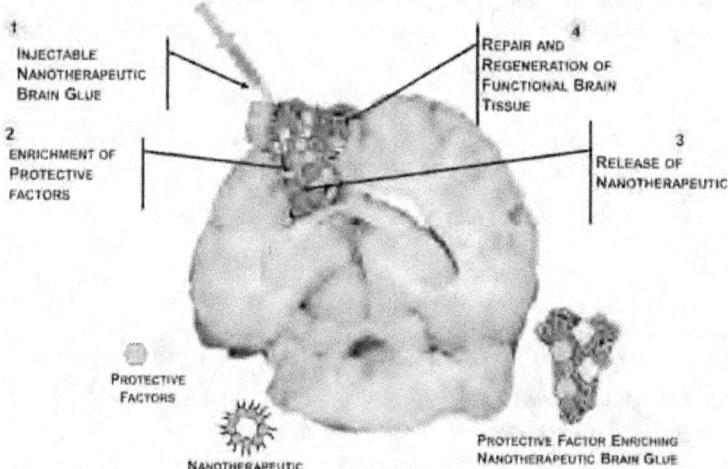

Closed-head and penetrating moderate-to-severe Traumatic Brain Injuries (TBIs) result in individuals suffering devastating loss of function and long-term disability due to the lack of available immediate (acute) treatment measures. Current interventions have failed to demonstrate measurable success. Our team at the University of Georgia's Regenerative Bioscience Center is focused on the development of novel nanotherapeutics that are derived from stem cells. This in combination with a novel "brain glue"[1] matrix has been formulated for the treatment of TBI. The proposed approach is novel because it can promote rapid wound healing of damaged brain tissue, and contains no cellular components that can complicate safe delivery. This formulation can be administered acutely after TBI and at the site of injury to: a) prevent progressive brain tissue damage by entrapping native protective factors and cells; b) Facilitate the protection and release of nanotherapeutic; and c) Promote long-term (chronic) functional recovery. Additionally, the state-of-the-art large animal research and veterinary capabilities available at the University of Georgia enable the testing of this formulation in a humanized pig model of TBI, which closely mimics human TBI. We also possess state-of-the-art gait analysis and video-tracking facilities[2], and resources to closely monitor the behavior and recovery of animals treated with nanotherapeutic laden brain glue constructs after TBI.

Our team at the University of Georgia consists of Dr. Steven L. Stice, an expert in stem cells and stem cell derived nanotherapeutics; Dr. Franklin West, an expert in developing humanized large animal models of TBI and stroke; and Dr. Lohitash Karumbaiah, an expert on material development for the treatment of brain and spinal cord injuries. Through this combined effort we hope to bridge the gap in the availability of acute treatments for moderate-to-severe TBI.

1 Simchick, G., Betancur M, **Karumbaiah L.** and Zhao Q. Gauging the Effectiveness of Traumatic Brain Injury Treatment using MR Phase Gradient Mapping. _Proceedings of the International Society for Magnetic Resonance in Medicine_ 2016 Singapore. p. 3420.

2 Duberstein KJ, Platt SR, Holmes SP, Dove CR, Howerth EW, Kent M, Stice SL, Hill WD, Hess DC, **West FD**. Gait analysis in a pre-and post-ischemic stroke biomedical pig model. _Physiology & behavior._ 2014 Feb 10;125:8-16.

www.ingramcontent.com/pod-product-compliance
Lightning Source LLC
Chambersburg PA
CBHW081243280526
45787CB00006B/2774